The Stress~Free Home

Beautiful Interiors for Serenity and Harmonious Living

ROCKPORT
PUBLISHERS

GLOUCESTER MASSACHUSETTS

Jackie Craven

First published in the United States of America by
Rockport Publishers, Inc.
33 Commercial Street
Gloucester, Massachusetts 01930-5089
Telephone: (978) 282-9590
Fax: (978) 283-2742
www.rockpub.com

Library of Congress Cataloging-in-Publication Data
Craven, Jackie.
   The stress-free home : beautiful interiors for serenity and harmonious
living / Jackie Craven.
      p.   cm.
   ISBN 1-59253-002-8 (hardcover)
   1. Interior decoration—Psychological aspects. I. Title.
NK2113.C744 2003
747'.01'9—dc21   2003002174

ISBN 1-59253-002-8

10 9 8 7 6 5 4 3 2 1

Design: Yee Design
Cover/Spine Image: Eric Roth
Back Cover Images: Courtesy of Zimmer + Rohoe, left and middle; Courtesty of R.O.O.M., right

Printed in China

Acknowledgments

The spirit of home and the comfort we find there is at the heart of any book on interior design. The talented designers and photographers whose work is reflected here capture that spirit, and I am deeply grateful.

For shepherding this project from inspiration to completion, I thank the entire team at Rockport Publishers, most especially Betsy Gammons, who never failed to find just the right photograph and to speak just the right words of encouragement. I am grateful to my agent, Barbara Doyen, for introducing us.

For twenty-five years of unwavering friendship and support, I thank all the members of my writer's group: Pauline Bartel, Joyce Bouyea, David Lee Drotar, Kate Kunz, Jane Streiff, and Donna Tomb.

Finally, my deepest appreciation goes to Susan Carroll Jewell, whose probing questions and original thought helped shape the direction of this book. Because of her professional research, invaluable writing, and eagle-eyed editing, the sometimes stressful job of working with words was for me a more wondrous and serene experience.

Contents

Chapter One

Patterns for Peaceful Living

**"This is the true nature of home—it is the place of Peace;
the shelter, not only from injury, but from all terror, doubt and division."**

John Ruskin (1819–1900), English author and art critic

Imagine a moment when you felt completely at peace. Perhaps you were strolling by a lake, kneeling in a temple, or relaxing on the porch of your childhood home. There were no ringing telephones, no petty quarrels, no pressing deadlines, no terrifying news reports. Worries slipped away and you seemed to merge with the flicker of light and shadow, the song of a bird, or the scent of lilacs. ▪ Sensations like these are all too fleeting. In a world of technological wonders, we are surrounded by uncertainties. We may be haunted by past events or anxious about what lies ahead. In the hectic pace of our lives, we often overlook the things that can bring us peace: the rhythm of falling rain, the bewitching interplay of color and pattern, the simple joys of kneading bread, stoking a fire, or rocking in a comfortable chair. ▪ A home designed for stress-free living evokes this type of serenity. Comfortable and convenient, beautiful and uncomplicated, it nurtures body, mind, and spirit. The design may begin with choosing restful colors, patterns, and shapes, yet these elements alone won't make a home tranquil. Creating peaceful, soothing environments involves the orchestration of many components, from the material details of fabrics and furnishings to the ethereal energies that all things possess. ▪ By combining these elements in ways that calm and delight, the stress-free home encourages love, camaraderie, and spiritual connectedness.

🌳 | **serenity secret #1**

Wrap yourself in softness. A cozy chenille throw, savored for its color and texture, can become your serenity blanket, recalling the comfort and safety you felt as a child. Save your serenity blanket for times when you especially need warmth and reassurance.

---

opposite *Serene spaces do not need to be minimalist or monochrome. Flowing draperies and carefully balanced colors bring a sense of tranquility to a cozy seating area.*

Designing for Serenity: two approaches

the Zen home	the stress-free home
Open spaces	Private spaces
White or neutral walls	Healing colors
Streamlined, functional furnishings	Ergonomic furnishings
Balanced, symmetrical arrangements	Soothing shapes and patterns
Natural fabrics and finishings	Eco-friendly materials
Minimal decorations	Carefully selected artifacts

opposite *The most restful bedrooms are uncomplicated. A firm mattress, pure cotton linens, and plenty of fresh air are all that's needed for a sound sleep.*

The Quest for Peace

Common sense tells us that every home should be relaxing and stress-free. Our homes are, after all, our shelter, our refuge, and the expression of our personalities and creativity. But, somewhere along the way, the ideal of home has become distorted. It's so easy to be swept away by fashion trends and enticing store window displays. Like tourists who have boarded the wrong bus, we may discover ourselves in a very different kind of home than the one we really need. We acquire chairs that cause backaches, collections that require dusting and polishing, carpeting that emits toxic fumes, entertainment centers that command our attention, electronics that click and beep and rattle our nerves, and books and papers that grow into weary piles of obligation. We spend countless hours cleaning and maintaining possessions that bring little joy, and everywhere we look, we are reminded of our frustrations and losses.

The quest for stress-free living has inspired a simpler, more orderly approach to decorating. Many designers have turned to the clean, uncluttered style drawn from the teachings of Zen Buddhism. In its most pure form, Zen design seeks escape from worldly worries. Furniture is selected for functionality and arranged with an eye toward symmetry and balance. Muted colors and expansive spaces encourage the tranquil state of self-forgetfulness. Earth-inspired patterns and textures, applied with restraint, express an appreciation for nature.

However, your home need not be monotone or minimalist to evoke a peaceful atmosphere. For many of us, peace comes not through self-forgetting but through self-remembering. You may feel more relaxed and more centered when you surround yourself with objects that express your cultural heritage. The desire for warm, comforting spaces may mean introducing plush cushions, a bright splash of color, and carefully chosen artifacts. The iron skillet Grandmother once used, the finger painting made by a child who is now grown, and a storybook from your own childhood provide important connections with the past and the future. While avoiding excess, truly peaceful environments remind us where we have been and where we are going.

right *A stress-free home will allow you to express your creativity and affirm cultural connections. The design is orderly and clutter-free, yet rich in details that have personal meaning. Here, a handcrafted footstool and woven carpets bring warmth and meaning to a symmetrical arrangement of matching chairs.*

serenity secret #2

Take comfort in a talisman. The ancients used crystals and amulets, but you need not believe in magic to feel the calming effect of a cherished object. Let a treasured heirloom or a favorite work of art serve as your symbol of safety and protection, bringing reassurance during times of stress.

Coping with Stress

As you plan your living space, your first step is to identify those things that sap your serenity and cause discord in your household. Sources of stress are all around us. Harsh music blaring from the house next door and pressures from an employer will easily arouse tensions and anxiety. A fluctuating stock market and news of terrorism or war can create an overwhelming sense of foreboding. Even a joyous event such as the birth of a child or an important career advance will stir up a tidal wave of emotions. Big events and minor nuisances, devastating losses and sudden successes will all lead to tightened muscles, rapid heartbeat, and other physiological symptoms we associate with stress.

All too frequently the things that distress us are circumstances we cannot control. We can, however, design living spaces that will help us cope with random world events, ease family conflicts, and calm the inner demons that kindle fear and discontent.

Make Easy Changes

Minimizing the impact of stressful events begins with identifying things you have control over and taking small, simple actions. Although you may not be able to alter political events, you can monitor how often you listen to the news. A chronic health problem may be beyond your control, but you still have the power to fill your home with soothing herbal fragrances. Sometimes even an unrelated action such as painting a door will bring a fresh outlook and open the way to new beginnings. Simply rearranging the furniture is healing, allowing you to shape your environment in meaningful ways.

Move Slowly

Changing the appearance or layout of your home is, in itself, potentially stressful. Instead of throwing the entire household into upheaval, work on one room or even a single corner. Instead of emptying a closet, clean out a single drawer. Be cautious about removing photographs and mementos. Memories that are painful to you now may be treasured years later. For an easier transition, remove sentimental items gradually and keep them in storage.

> "I too am a rare
> Pattern... As I wander down
> The garden-paths."
>
> Amy Lowell (1874–1925), American poet

Work from the Inside Out

The atmosphere of a room is more than the sum of its decor. Things we
cannot explain or even name will exert subtle influence on your emotional
state. To create spaces where you will feel at peace, listen closely to your
instincts and choose details that resonate for you. Consider all the senses:
sight, sound, scent, touch, and taste. Also, do not forget subtle environmental influences such as temperature, humidity, lighting, and ventilation.

Involve the Entire Family

Designing for serenity is a personal process, but it affects much more than
the self. Through the harmonious arrangement of colors, patterns, and
shapes we hope to encourage harmony in our relationships. Every being in
the household—children, pets, and aging parents—will be impacted by
seemingly insignificant details in the environment. Designing living areas
and other shared spaces will call for friendly negotiations and carefully considered compromises. One person's passion for plush cushions may yield to
another's appreciation for sleek metallics, while fabrics and wallcoverings
may incorporate the favorite colors of several family members.

Design Guidelines

There are no rigid rules for designing a stress-free environment. We each
draw comfort and strength from different sources. The answers for you
may lie in ancient Eastern philosophies or in classical principles of design.
You may be intrigued by the findings of modern psychologists only to return,
once again, to lessons you learned from your grandmother. Creating a
stress-free home is a journey of exploration and self-discovery. Use these
guidelines as a starting point for creating spaces that bring you tranquility.

Floor Plans

The most serene environments acknowledge fundamental human needs
for space and privacy. Designing a stress-free home may mean rethinking
the placement of rooms and furnishings. Expansive, open areas will evoke
a sense of freedom, but cozy, comforting nooks are often preferred for
relaxation and meditation. Comfort and convenience are key when planning rooms. Modern theories of ergonomics encourage stress-free living

above *Natural sunlight, earth-inspired colors, and bowls of fresh fruit make the kitchen a pleasing area to celebrate simple comforts.*

"Reduce big troubles to small ones, and small ones to nothing."

Chinese proverb

Tranquility Tools

Vástu Shástra:
Follow guidelines from ancient India for harmonious floor plans and furniture arrangements.

Feng Shui:
Balance the flow of energies according to ancient Chinese philosophies.

Celestial Design:
Look to the stars and find inspiration in early tribal customs.

Spiritual Geometry:
Seek archetypal shapes and patterns that express a sense of universal order.

Hydrotherapy:
Celebrate the healing power of water in home spas and other indoor waterspaces.

Aromatherapy:
Use healing aromas from fresh flowers, dried herbs, and essential oils.

Color Therapy:
Choose colors for their proven ability to affect emotions and physical well-being.

Light Therapy:
Flood rooms with the healing rays of full-spectrum lighting.

Air and Water Purifiers:
Free the home from stress-inducing pollutants.

Sound Conditioners:
Mask distracting outside noise with soothing music and sounds drawn from nature.

Gestalt Psychology:
Explore the deeper emotional contexts of rooms and their decor.

Jungian Analysis:
Make meaningful symbols the focal point for your rooms.

through easy-reach storage, step-saving furniture arrangements, and seating that promotes healthy posture. Many designers also look to *feng shui, vástu shástra,* and other ancient philosophies for ideas on ways to redirect the flow of energy through the home.

Shapes and Lines

Every room is unique, expressing the personalities and values of those who live there. Nevertheless, we all have a seemingly inborn need for what is often called the "universal principles of design." Our sense of unity, proportion, and balance will often determine whether a room feels "right." An undersized painting on a long, blank wall can create an undercurrent of unrest. A single, heavy armoire at the far end of a room can make the space feel lopsided, upsetting our equilibrium. However, the need for balance and order does not mean that our homes must be perfectly symmetrical. Instead, you are likely to discover a great deal of quiet excitement in the subtle interplay of line, shape, form, and pattern. An inviting grouping of chairs or an exquisite collection of pottery can provide a satisfying counterpoint to other items in the room.

Sensual Details

Numerous studies have shown that color and light will trigger strong physiological and emotional responses. Peaceful rooms make full use of mood-enhancing light from the Sun or from specially designed full-spectrum fixtures. Healing colors, noted for their calming effects, are drawn from earth, sea, and sky. Other sensual details, selected for their soothing properties and medicinal powers, add richness and texture to the atmosphere. The gentle notes of a wind chime, the restful scent of lavender, and, perhaps, even the energizing taste of strawberries become as important to the room as its furnishings.

Physical Health

A peaceful mind begins with a healthy body; a serene living space will nurture and protect the physical well-being of all who enter. Natural fabrics and finishes are preferred not only because they are beautiful but also because they are free of formaldehyde and other toxic chemicals. Uncomplicated and comforting bedcovers are made from unbleached, untreated cotton. Plush woolen area rugs or grassy sisal floor mats replace synthetic wall-to-wall carpeting. Warm, natural sunlight and lush aromas become an important part of the design because they please the senses and also have a proven power to heal.

Nature and Technology

No home is an island. It must exist in a larger environment and it must utilize natural resources. A peaceful dwelling is eco-friendly. The use of biodegradable and recycled materials expresses a reverence for nature. Flourishing plant life and indoor fountains reflect spiritual ties with the natural world. Appliances are selected for their compact shapes and their energy efficiency. Computers, televisions, and other electronics are incorporated in pleasing, unobtrusive ways.

Artifacts

There is no question that clutter rattles our nerves and drains our spirits. As you re-create your home, you and your family will want to seek ways to clear away or sensibly store papers, books, and odd assortments of knick-knacks. Designing tranquil spaces is a process of deciding what is important and what is not. Consequently, home design becomes a deep and gradual process of self-analysis. Art and artifacts that have personal meaning or symbolic significance become key elements in the design of a home that is truly serene.

As You Begin . . .

Serenity is expressed through things we can see—colors, patterns, and shapes—but it is also sensed through the heart. A stress-free home encourages inner calm and spiritual enlightenment. It fosters peaceful relations between life partners, reaffirms connections with nature, and expresses caring and respect for the environment.

Take inspiration from the serene rooms photographed here and pause for quiet reflection. Think about favorite places from your past and beautiful rooms you've only imagined. Write down your dreams, or draw pictures and floor plans for the home you would like to create. As you begin to make small changes, notice how the atmosphere shifts. Talk with family and friends, and decide which strategies work best for you. Serenity does not come with a flash or a boom but with a gradual warming of the spirit. Let it begin now.

"True life is lived when tiny changes occur."

Leo Tolstoy (1828–1910), Russian author

🌳 | **serenity secret #4**

Paint your bathroom blue. Pale, watery colors vibrate at frequencies you'll find naturally soothing. For deep relaxation, sprinkle your bathwater with lavender oil and bathe in the silvery blue hue of moonlight.

opposite *Tucked in a narrow alcove, a tranquil bathing area evokes the atmosphere of sky and sea. The hand spray allows for soothing hydromassage.*

Chapter Two

Ancient Wisdoms

All things in the universe are composed of energy; endlessly rotating electrons and neutrons make up every living thing, every object, every swirling gas and grain of dust. Modern physicists are only just beginning to unlock the mysteries of energy and matter, but philosophers have been exploring these concepts since before the dawn of recorded history. In some cultures, ruminations about the forces of nature have evolved into sophisticated guidelines for aligning energies and achieving order and balance in our lives. ▪

Perhaps the best-known philosophies are *feng shui,* originating in China, and *vástu shástra,* originating in India. Both philosophies teach that electrical, magnetic, and gravitational forces influence every aspect of human activity. For the uninitiated, the theories may seem strange and incomprehensible, yet both *feng shui* and *vástu shástra* offer specific, practical advice for the placement of rooms, furnishings, and decorative details. Their teachings suggest reasons why some rooms feel cold and uninviting while others lift our spirits, why the baby wakes in the night, and why the cat tears through the house as though its tail was on fire. Moreover, these philosophies offer solutions—often minor adjustments in room decoration—to resolve conflicts and restore harmony.

🌳 | **serenity secret #5**

Check your *chi.* Frequent quarrels or emotional upsets could be due to an excess of *yang* energy in the passionate southern portion of your home, say *feng shui* pratitioners. Place a large clay pot filled with yellow primroses in that area. The *yin* energy of the earthen clay and the flowers will help stabilize the energies and encourage family harmony. At the very least, they'll cheer you up.

---

opposite *Ancient Chinese warriors used reflective armor to deflect hostile energies and protect themselves from harm. Modern* feng shui *practitioners often use mirrors to channel energies through the home. To avoid "beheading" viewers, choose mirrors that are very tall.*

"The most beautiful thing we can experience is the mysterious."

Albert Einstein (1879–1955), German-born U.S. physicist

Dual Energies

yin design	**yang** design
To create stress-free rooms, choose shapes, colors, and textures that contain tranquil *yin* energy.	For home offices, kitchens, and other high-activity areas, choose shapes, colors, and textures that contain stimulating *yang* energy.
Thin, wavy lines	Straight or angular lines
Blue, green, and pastel colors	Red and orange
Soft carpeting	Glass, marble, and stone
Flowing drapery	Wooden or metal window blinds
Cushioned furniture	Unupholstered furnishings

opposite *According to* feng shui *beliefs, the curved shape and padded cushions give this chair a quiet* yin *quality, making it conducive for relaxation and meditation. The red pillow, however, is* yang, *which suggests fire energy and promotes fame and power. Together, these* yin yang *forces invite both alertness and concentration.*

Feng shui and *vástu shástra* date back thousands of years, but, even before these systems were developed, prehistoric peoples observed the heavens and theorized that mystical life energies, controlled by the movement of the Sun, Moon, and stars, shaped the happiness and well-being of every individual. In all parts of the world, tribes have developed rituals and symbols to help members harmonize with natural forces and thereby improve their emotional and psychological well-being.

Today, few of us remember our ties to the earth; we are often unaware of planetary movements and we do not consider the powerful energies that all things possess. Our spirits may resemble wildly swinging pendulums, unable to find the quiet still point at the center. Revisiting ancient and prehistoric beliefs is one way to reconnect with natural forces and to rediscover the things that bring us the greatest level of peace and joy.

Feng Shui

Feng shui is not one philosophy but many. The complex system of ideas began in China and spread through Tibet and the rest of Asia. Over the course of six thousand years, the tools and techniques expanded to include a broad range of ideas and approaches. At its most basic level, *feng shui* (meaning *wind/water*) offers ways to channel life energies (called *chi*). According to *feng shui* teachings, all things in the universe are made up of two polar energies, *yin* and *yang*. A profoundly restful environment has more *yin* energy: every aspect of the decor encourages peace or introspection. A room that excites and inspires is predominantly *yang:* the decor promotes activity and extroversion. However, both *yin* and *yang* are essential to life, and the goal of *feng shui* is to achieve a harmonious balance between the two.

"Just remain in the center, watching.
And then forget that you are there."

Lau-Tzu (604–531 B.C.), Chinese spiritual leader

Feng Shui Tips

- *Consult a ba-gua chart to find the most favorable energy centers.*

- *Clear away clutter, meaningless collections, and unused furnishings.*

- *Seek balance in furniture arrangements.*

- *Use lighting, mirrors, crystals, and chimes to direct the flow of energy.*

- *Use plants to soften sharp, jutting angles and to energize stagnant corners.*

- *Make sure all doors and windows open easily, even if you never use them.*

- *Choose natural materials for fabrics, furnishings, floors, and countertops.*

- *Repair leaking faucets promptly.*

- *Make sure water in flower vases, fountains, and fish tanks is fresh.*

To achieve this, some practitioners look closely at surrounding geographic features such as mountains, streams, buildings, and roads. Others use a compass to determine the most favorable directions according to precise mathematical calculations. Today, many *feng shui* followers take an eclectic approach, combining the ancient laws with color healing, astrology, and an assortment of modern tools such as air ionizers and electromagnetic radiation detectors.

Regardless of the approach used, designing your home according to *feng shui* principles means paying close attention to the flow of *chi* through its rooms and fine-tuning your instincts for what "feels right." You may want to seek advice from a trained *feng shui* practitioner (a *geomancer*), or you may choose to merely sample the ancient Chinese art. Even minor changes made according to *feng shui* guidelines can make a dramatic difference in the atmosphere your home evokes.

Ba-gua Basics

In this simplified version of the ba-gua, no compass is required. Simply align the bottom of the chart with your front door. Then, observe where the energy centers fall in relationship to the rooms in your home.

wealth and prosperity	fame and success	love and marriage
family	wholeness and health	children and creativity
learning and knowledge	career	helpful people

opposite *Modern design mingles with ancient wisdoms in this sleek, efficient kitchen. The sink is placed away from the stove, assuring harmony between fire and water elements. Smooth, rounded work surfaces invite a smooth flow of energy.*

below *Cherished by the ancients, sunlight, water, and blooming foliage combine to create a deeply soothing bathing area.*

The *Ba-gua*

A helpful tool used by many *feng shui* believers is the *ba-gua*. This eight-sided diagram is derived from the *I-Ching,* the Chinese book of Divination, and serves as an energy map for your home. Each side of the diagram represents a different aspect of life and suggests the most favorable locations for important daily activities. There are many variations of the *ba-gua;* some specify compass directions while others simply show where your home's energy centers fall in relation to your front door. Regardless of the method used, the goal is to identify the areas in your home where energies are strong, and areas that need "energy adjustments." Once you have this knowledge, you can employ a variety of *feng shui* cures.

Vástu Shástra

When you explore *vástu shástra,* you move even farther back in time than *feng shui.* Thousands of years ago, before *feng shui* evolved in China, Hindus in India taught that our dwellings should exist in harmony with nature and the universe. The sacred Hindu scriptures, the *Vedas,* set forth a series of design principles known as *vástu shástra,* also called *sthapatya ved,* or *Vedic* design. Drawing upon *jyotish* (Indian astrology), the principles describe the planetary forces on the natural elements and, consequently, on worldly circumstances. Creating a stress-free environment means aligning those forces so that the dweller, the dwelling, and the cosmos are in harmony.

At first glance, *vástu shástra* may seem similar to *feng shui.* Both philosophies seek harmony by removing obstructions and enhancing the flow of natural energies. Both find power in five primary elements and both emphasize the importance of planetary alignment for harmonious

above *Pleasing natural illumination and convenient floor plans are hallmarks of vástu design. In keeping with ancient beliefs, the painting depicts a soothing, natural scene.*

Vástu Tips

- *Prepare a* jyotish *(astrological) chart.*

- *Arrange rooms according to favorable planetary alignments.*

- *Make sure doors open smoothly and swing inward.*

- *Choose nontoxic, eco-friendly fabrics and furnishings.*

- *Keep central spaces and passageways open.*

- *Set furniture and appliances slightly away from the walls.*

- *Echo two or three favorite colors through the entire house.*

- *Provide opportunities for abundant sunlight.*

- *Decorate abundantly with living foliage.*

right *A harmonious balance of fire and earth are reflected in this serene seating arrangement. Growing foliage flanks the fireplace and, in keeping with vástu teachings, the space around the chair is free of obstructions.*

placement of rooms and furnishings. However, each philosophy is deeply rooted in the culture where it was conceived and places different layers of meaning on objects and their placement.

A home designed according to *Vedic* guidelines seeks to inspire profound pleasure and inner peace by affirming the unity between all things. Rooms and furnishings that follow essential laws of nature will bring calm and fulfillment. Rooms that defy these laws are likely to provoke stress, anxiety, or depression. The rules of *vástu* are complex; however, they can be customized. Drawing upon *ayurveda*, a system of holistic health practices, the *vástu* practitioner will consider the physical and psychological elements that make up the consitution, or *dosha*, of each family member. Harmony is achieved by aligning needs of the individual with forces of nature and movement of the stars.

The *vástu* designer plays many roles, from astrologer to psychotherapist, philosopher to medical doctor. Special attention is paid to the placement of rooms and furnishings in orientation to the Sun. Harmony is expressed through a pleasing flow of colors, patterns, and textures. Abundant plant life and natural materials such as cotton, sisal, and wood affirm our connection with nature. Setting aside a special area of the home for *puja*, or worship, honors spiritual needs.

"I have ceased to question stars and books; I have begun to listen to the teaching my blood whispers to me."

Herman Hesse (1877–1962), German author

Celestial Design

Long before civilizations evolved in China and India, tribes in all parts of the world recognized the forces of the Sun, Moon, and stars. With ties close to the earth, early peoples centered their lives around seasonal planting and harvesting, cycles of the Moon, and changes in the weather. A spiritual leader, shaman, or medicine man found power and enlightenment in the wind, rain, lightning, and other forces of nature.

Many tribes honored nature's rhythms by constructing a large stone circle on a sacred site, often between intersecting rivers or on mountaintops. Perhaps the most famous of these structures is Stonehenge, a megalith monument in England. However, similar constructions have been found in every part of the world, from Egypt to Tibet to the remote Easter Island. In North and South America, some tribes created "medicine wheels"—circular arrangements of stones with radiating spokes to mark the Sun's directions or to symbolize the passage of time.

Prehistoric stone circles symbolized life as an endless cycle and also illustrated the interconnectedness of all things in the universe. The circle became a physical manifestation of natural forces and defined a spiritual space where healing and transformation could occur. During rituals and important ceremonies, the circle provided a place for tribespeople to move symbolically through stages of psychological and spiritual development. Some Native American tribes marked their stone circles with animal carvings and other symbolic objects that represented life energies.

The ancient symbols and rituals are, for the most part, lost in time. Nevertheless, we can draw much wisdom from the ancient practice of assigning energies and meanings to circular patterns and the cycles of Sun and Moon. Your house will become your own personal medicine wheel when you put special thought into where you place significant objects. Place a ceramic bird, representing spirituality and creativity, near an eastern window where it catches the first light of the rising Sun. Set aside a quiet northern corner for photo albums and leather-bound books. By honoring treasured mementos, you will begin to nourish your values, aspirations, and dreams.

🌳 | serenity secret #6

Gaze at the stars. Think about how far away they are and how many years their light traveled to reach our planet. Your own problems will seem less important as you contemplate the universe.

---

opposite *African artifacts evoke a sense of timelessness in an open living space. The limited palate unifies the eclectic collection.*

Lessons from the Inca

In the remote Andes mountain range of South America, the Inca created vast stone circles according to a plan that has been handed down to their descendants. Representing natural rhythms and life energies, these stone circles, or medicine wheels, incorporated symbols and icons important in the daily life of the tribe. Carvings and other artifacts were both beautiful and powerful because they were drawn from deeply cherished ideals. Use the Inca medicine wheel as inspiration, but choose your own images to represent your most treasured values and dreams.

South: The Serpent (Sachamama). South is the direction for healing and renewal. Just as a snake slithers from its skin, we will shed the past. Although we do not forget our failures and losses, we are no longer bound by them and we are free to make new choices. The south is, therefore, an ideal location for bedrooms, bathrooms, and other places where we seek restoration.

West: The female jaguar. The west is the direction where we can best face our fears. Moving like a jaguar with grace and power, we will look death in the eye and see it not as an ending but as a transformation. In the same way, we will take inventory of our weaknesses and find quiet peace with ourselves. Kitchens, home offices, and other busy work areas are ideally placed in the west.

North: The white horse, the white buffalo, the dragon, or the hummingbird. North is where learning and wisdom occur. You will receive guidance from your ancestors and accept the collective wisdom of the human race. You may want to use the northern corner of your home for reading and study.

East: The eagle and the condor. The east is the direction of profound insight. Just as *vástu shástra* philosophies teach that we should face east when we pray and when we sleep, the Inca associated the rising Sun with spiritual awakening. With the keen vision of an eagle or a condor, we will see beyond material things and discover our true potential. Place meditation rooms or personal shrines in the eastern corner of the home.

right *Prehistoric tribal customs suggest that we can achieve harmony with the universe through the careful placement of treasured objects. In this bright living area, earthen pots are arranged in orderly rows on an upper ledge. Soft, inviting chairs surround an unassuming woven bowl.*

"May serenity circle on silent wings and catch the whisper of the wind."

Cheewa James, contemporary Native American author, Modoc tribe

serenity secret #8

Name one fear. Write it on a scrap of paper. Place the paper in a deep, flameproof bowl and set it on fire. Envision your fear drifting away with the smoke.

Answers from the Past

Exploring the belief systems of early cultures can be enlightening and transforming. Each offers its own unique perspective on how we can create environments that are in harmony with natural forces. While the philosophies differ and often contradict one another, they all teach that the objects in our daily lives are important and that the way we choose to arrange them will have an enormous impact on our physical and emotional well-being.

Choose a philosophy that reflects your cultural heritage or that resonates for you. Learn the ancient laws and follow them faithfully or simply draw on the ideas you find most useful. Don't be afraid to mingle philosophical approaches. You may choose to arrange the floor plan of your home according to a *feng shui ba-gua*, create a traditional Hindu *puja* room, and incorporate symbols drawn from Inca ideology. Or, you may do nothing more than hang a mirror to draw energy into a dingy room. Even shifting the location of a single chair will alter the atmosphere in your home. Let your instincts be a barometer: You will know that you are on the right path when you believe that change is possible.

opposite *Contemporary furnishings mingle with ancient wisdoms in this nature-loving space. Floppy, charmingly oversized leaves and a cluster of gourds celebrate life with joyful exuberance.*

Chapter Three

Space and Movement

"We shape our buildings. Thereafter they shape us."
Winston Churchill (1874–1965), British statesman

The floor plans of our homes are the blueprints of our lives. We circle the dining table, sidestep the settee, and pace back and forth between the kitchen and family room. The way we organize our living spaces determines the amount of effort needed to complete basic household chores, affects our interaction with family members, and shapes the emotional quality of our days. ▪ Stress-free homes invite free and easy movement. Rooms and furnishings are arranged to avoid conflicts and collisions. Functionality and flexibility are key. Doors swing open smoothly, passageways are well-lit, chairs are comfortable and practical, and individual needs for space and privacy are accommodated. Rooms and furnishings are easily accessible for family members and visitors with disabilities. The home is easy to clean and maintain because clutter is eliminated and storage is conveniently located. Family disputes are avoided because busy activity centers are clearly defined and logically placed. Spaces are designed to encourage their primary functions: recreation areas invite play, office areas inspire productive work, and bedrooms enhance sleep and intimacy. ▪ Creating a more peaceful environment may mean reshaping the floor plan of your home, moving activities to different rooms, rearranging furnishings, and finding new purposes for underutilized areas. Or, you may discover that just a few minor adjustments will shift the flow of traffic in helpful ways. To determine troublespots, take a careful inventory of your entire home. Be sure to explore all the rooms, including unfinished areas such as the attic, basement, and storage areas.

🌳 | **serenity secret #9**

Reflect. Remember a time you felt perfectly at peace. Close your eyes and visualize your chosen place in detail. Where are you? What colors do you see? What shapes and textures? Do you hear music or other sounds? Can you sense a special aroma? Make a list of these details and begin incorporating them into your home.

---

opposite *A folding screen helps define a private area for quiet relaxation.*

Survey Your Space

opposite *A deep bathtub with a reading rack and a wall display of botanical prints transforms a tiny bathroom into a peaceful getaway.*

below *In a rustic space, festoons of white cotton gauze create a romantic, restful, and private retreat.*

Identify the areas that feel crowded and cluttered.

Observe the places where clutter accumulates: the tables that are often piled with papers and projects, the rumbled clothing tossed across chairs, the tangle of boots blocking the stairs. See the telltale fingerprints on the wall. Clues like these will reveal which parts of your home are most highly trafficked.

Sense the emotional tenor of each room.

Take a careful emotional inventory of the spaces and their furnishings. You may draw upon ancient philosophies such as *feng shui,* or listen closely to your internal sense of what feels right. Identify the areas where family and visitors gravitate and the areas that are seldom used. Look for the sore spots and the joyful places. Watch for laughter, tears, squabbles, and expressions of affection; make note where they most frequently occur.

Observe environmental conditions.

Take time to listen closely to what your dwelling is telling you. Examine the fixed structural elements: the size and shape of the room, the height of the ceiling, the size and placement of the windows, and the presence of support beams and important decorative details such as columns, mantels, and built-in shelving. Walk through each room at various times of the day and night; observe the movement of the Sun and the shifting light and shadow. Make note of sounds, aromas, and physical sensations. Check the temperature and the humidity. A warm, bright room near a bustling kitchen can be an ideal location for socializing, while a small, windowless space may be best suited for reading or meditation. A room that is too damp or chilly for most uses can often provide much-needed space for exercise equipment or laundry machines.

Honor your house.

In many ways, our dwellings tell us what they want to be. Despite our fondest wishes for an office adjacent to the kitchen or a secluded library in the basement, conditions in those spaces may make our dreams impractical. Moreover, the architectural style of the building and the topography of the surrounding landscape may suggest a personality that will become a part of the family dynamic. Imagine your home as a person. Is it male or female? Quiet or boisterous? Serious or frivolous? Allow this unique personality to find expression in the arrangement and design of its rooms.

"Always keep a place to which you can retreat."

Chinese proverb

opposite *An attic alcove flooded with sunlight is an ideal getaway for painting, writing, and other creative activities. Plenty of cross-ventilation keeps the space from becoming too warm.*

right *Bunk beds tucked into the eaves provide plenty of sleeping space for children and teens. Plush carpeting helps muffle sounds of noisy play and music.*

Know Your Needs

Each of us has a sense of territory. Sometimes these feelings are spoken: "my kitchen," "my workshop," "my desk." More frequently, we are not consciously aware of the possessiveness we feel for places and things. Acknowledging territorial needs is important because they are so often the source of tension and conflict. Sparks will certainly fly when two children feel they "own" the chair by the window. And, although two adults are not likely to come to blows over the bathroom vanity, unpleasantness will mount if they both feel they are entitled to it. As you reshape the space inside your home, you will want to make sure that each family member, including the smallest child, has a special area to call her own.

Plan for the future.

No family is immune to the forces of change. The home you plan today will be quite different from the one you'll need in the years ahead. Perhaps a flourishing business will clamor for more space, or your household may expand to include a new baby or an aging parent. Try to anticipate these changes now and your family will not be thrown into upheaval later on. Lightweight furnishings and neutral colors will permit rooms to quickly adapt to changing needs.

Make room for dreams.

Don't limit yourself to the merely pragmatic as you plan the rooms in your home. When you give an activity—or an idea—space, you acknowledge its importance and you open the way for possibilities. If you have always yearned to be a writer, set aside an area devoted to writing. Ignore the cautious and critical voices. Now is the time to design the inspiring kitchen for the aspiring gourmet cook and the attic studio for the teenager who loves to paint. By giving dreams room, you encourage them to become realities.

Create New Spaces

Ultimately, every designer must work within the boundaries of existing walls. Unless you are building a new home or doing extensive remodeling, you will need to find innovative ways to use the space you have right now. Begin with the forgotten spaces, the areas that often sit empty. Look for creative ways to utilize the attic, basement, laundry room, and garage. A damp basement may be the ideal setting for a home spa and exercise center; a heated garage could be the best spot for noisy music practice. Don't forget the small, out-of-the way nooks. The places that comfort us are often cozy and sheltered. With a lamp and a few pillows, a window alcove or a recess beneath the stairs can become a private haven.

Next, seek the rooms that are underutilized. A guestroom that is rarely visited may offer possibilities for an art studio. A dining room that sits idle can become a dynamic home theater. If children need more space for toys and play, consider giving them the master bedroom. The key is to think beyond the predictable and allow rooms to take on new, unexpected roles. As you explore possibilities, remember to look outdoors. When weather is warm, consider using the porch or deck for dining and socializing. Create a private courtyard surrounded by hedges, or turn a gazebo or pergola into an open-air living room. Sturdy and comfortable wooden furnishings and soft, colorful cushions will help assure that the outdoor area is well utilized. Playful and romantic touches such as a Persian carpet or a wingback chair will add to the illusion that your yard is an extension of your living room.

Light and color will alter the way any space is perceived, making it appear smaller or larger than it is in reality. Sunlight, natural views, and

"If there is room in your heart, there is room in your house."

Danish proverb

opposite *During warm weather, let the porch or patio become an extension of your living room. Lighthearted details such as a chandelier suspended from a tree branch help blur the boundaries between indoors and out.*

pastel colors—especially whites and powder blues—create the illusion of openness. To expand your space, replace bulky curtains with lightweight bamboo shades and paint walls pale, neutral tones. Install a skylight or sliding glass doors to capture life-affirming sunlight, or use bright, diffused artificial lighting to broaden the boundaries of the room. To define cozy, intimate spaces, place small lamps beside comfortable seating areas. The golden halo of incandescent bulbs will help establish a sense of privacy.

The Japanese
Nihon-ma

The traditional Japanese room, or nihon-ma, is an open and airy space that is easily reshaped according to need.

- **Fusuma:** *translucent sliding doors to partition interior spaces*

- **Shoji:** *translucent sliding doors, usually in sets of four, to separate interior from exterior spaces*

- **Ranma:** *decorative transoms for ventilation*

- **Tatami:** *rice-straw floor mats*

- **Zabuton:** *seating cushions*

- **Tokonoma:** *an alcove or corner where treasured items are placed*

- **Tokobashira:** *wooden or bamboo pillars supporting the tokonoma*

left *A contemporary cherry onda (wave) bed and a wardrobe made of translucent sliding screens capture the serene atmosphere of a traditional Japanese nihon-ma.*

above *Portable furnishings will bring new uses to forgotten spaces. All you need is a folding chair and a lightweight table to transform a utility room or enclosed porch into a quiet retreat.*

"The art of life is a constant readjustment to our surroundings."

Kakuzo Okakaura (1862–1913), Japanese philosopher and author

Easy Movement

The term *ergonomics* is often used when describing office furnishings, but the science is a broad one that applies to every part of our built environment. It involves choosing furnishings, lighting, color, and other details that will minimize stress on our bodies and reduce the amount of effort needed to complete tasks. Consider how many steps will be needed to prepare and serve meals, supervise children, and answer phone calls. Be sure to store items close to where they will be used and avoid placing frequently used items on high shelves. Simply placing the television remote within easy reach will do much to minimize frustrations and keep peace in the family.

High-traffic areas like living rooms, television rooms, and playrooms need to be comfortable and flexible. Choose recliners rather than sofas; they are more relaxing for reading and watching television and can also be relocated more easily. In Italian, the word for furniture is *mobilia*, suggesting that tables, chairs, and other furnishings should not be fixed in place. Practical, portable furnishings open possibilities for any room, letting you alter space to meet changing needs.

Take inspiration from the traditional Japanese *nihon-ma*. Furnished entirely with cushions, mats, lightweight tables, and translucent screens, these airy spaces can be transformed at a moment's notice. You can achieve this type of fluidity simply by removing heavy, ponderous furnishings and discarding nonessentials. Tables with drop leaves and nested tables help clear floor space. Furniture on casters will easily roll to new locations. After spending time in relaxed, flexible spaces, you may notice a certain sense of buoyancy. The freedom to move the furniture can lead to other, less tangible freedoms. Rearranging the living room becomes a way to invite transformation into your life.

Universal Design

A home that minimizes stress is appealing and comfortable for people of all ages with a wide range of abilities. Even when everyone in the family is able-bodied, it is understood that some visitors may have mobility problems or visual impairments that could make parts of the home inaccessible, if not designed with sensitivity. Moreover, a sudden accident or the long-term effects of illness or aging could make mobility increasingly difficult for anyone in the household. Universal design means creating spaces that meet the needs of all people, young and old, able and disabled. Detailed guidelines are readily available from governmental housing agencies and a variety of other sources. Listed here are a few general concepts to think about as you plan your rooms.

opposite *A stress-free home enables easy movement for all people, young and old, abled and disabled. Combining beauty with functionality, this pleasant room provides several types of seating, assuring the comfort of family and visitors with differing needs.*

Designing Accessible Spaces

- *Allow enough floor space to accommodate a stationary wheelchair and also enough room for a smooth U turn: at least 198 cm (78 inches) by 152 cm (60 inches).*

- *Include tables or counters that are a variety of heights to accommodate standing, seating, and a range of different tasks.*

- *Provide shelves and a medicine cabinet that can be reached by persons seated in a wheelchair.*

- *Make sure entry doors to rooms are at least 81 cm (32 inches) wide.*

- *Mount bathroom sinks no higher than 86 cm (34 inches) from the floor.*

- *Install grab bars in the shower and beside the toilet.*

- *Provide a full-length mirror that can be viewed by all people, including children.*

- *Avoid shag carpets, uneven brick floors, and other floor surfaces that could pose slipping and tripping hazards.*

"Men cannot see their reflection in running water, but only in still water. Only that which is itself still can still the seekers of stillness."

Chuang Tzu (369?–268 B.C.), Chinese Taoist philosopher

Spiritual Spaces

For many families, serenity is rooted in a deep sense of spirituality. To foster an attitude of reverence, a special area is set aside for worship and meditation. Some Buddhist families dedicate space for a *zendo*, or meditation area. Hindu homes frequently incorporate a *puja*, or prayer room. Other faiths practice a variety of traditions, decorating their spiritual spaces with carefully chosen symbols and artifacts.

Doctors and researchers attest to the importance of following some type of spiritual activity. Meditation and prayer will not necessarily resolve problems, but taking time for quiet reflection does lower blood pressure and remove many symptoms of stress. Regardless of your faith, you may want to designate a special "serenity zone" in your home. An attic, an unfinished basement, and even a closet can become a sanctuary provided that the space is comfortable and apart from the noisy bustle of the household.

Your spirituality center need not be a place for formal religious practice, but it can help you and other members of the household pause, reconsider priorities, and rediscover the things that are truly important. Bring in artwork that represents your beliefs, fill elegant vases with fresh peonies, or set seashells on a shelf to remind you of deep oceans and rolling waves. Choosing the colors and accessories for this space can become a meaningful family activity, prompting each member of the household to clarify values and discover common bonds.

opposite *A small table with candles and a few treasured objects can become a stabilizing force in the home, providing a quiet place for prayer and meditation.*

Find Peace through Meditation

Our minds are always busy. As we go about our daily lives, we are also planning, worrying, ruminating, and anticipating. Meditation is a way to settle down the stormy seas of thought. Since ancient times, Eastern religions such as Buddhism and Hinduism have used meditation as a way to rise above worldly concerns and elevate awareness of the cosmic whole. Although traditional techniques require many years of study, you can begin meditating right now simply by focusing your attention on a single thing— an object, a mental image, a word, or your own breathing. In this way, you will help calm your busy thoughts and may quickly feel a profound sense of relaxation. If you would like to learn a formal meditation practice, you might want to begin with one of these:

serenity secret #12

Seek the still place inside yourself. Inhale deeply to a count of ten, then slowly exhale, also to a count of ten. Close your eyes and listen. Imagine that your breath is the wind whirling through you, blowing away all thoughts and worries. Feel the movement deep in your abdomen, and know that you are strong.

- **Vipassana, or Buddhist Mindfulness Meditation**

  As you concentrate closely on an object, image, or a sound, you will observe passing thoughts and sensations without judging or analyzing. Doing this will lead you toward a calm, nonreactive Zen state of mind.

- **Transcendental Meditation (TM)**

  You will use a mantra—a repeated word or phrase—to promote deep relaxation. Any thoughts that rise to the surface of your mind are acknowledged and then gently pushed aside.

- **Visualization Meditation**

  Breathing deeply, you will visualize light or color or healing energy moving to various parts of your body. By doing this, you will ease tension, relieve pain, and promote healing.

- **Moving Meditation**

  Yoga, tai chi, and many other traditions use motion as a means toward enlightenment. Under the guidance of a master, you will learn specific postures, movements, and breathing techniques to unify mind, body, and spirit.

Chapter Four

Balance and Order

". . . No building can be said to be well designed which wants symmetry and proportion.
In truth they are as necessary to the beauty of a building as to that of a well-formed human figure."

Vitruvius (30 B.C. to A.D. 14), Roman architect

The human spirit longs for balance and order. Our own bodies are, after all, evenly proportioned with two eyes, two ears, two arms, and two legs on each side. When studied under the microscope, our cells reveal a highly ordered system of shapes and patterns, the same system found in every part of nature from swimming fish to swirling planets. Instinctively, we are calmed and reassured by environments that reflect nature's geometry. ▪ Builders of long ago knew this and sought to design spaces that were symmetrical and highly ordered. Structures like the Pyramids of Egypt, the temples of ancient Greece and Rome, the Mayan monuments, Europe's grand gothic cathedrals, and India's Taj Mahal are deeply satisfying because they express a reverence for fundamental principles of balance, order, and proportion. Although every building is a unique work of art, each echoes the archetypal forms that are the blueprints for all life. Early builders often assigned spiritual meanings to shapes and forms and to the ratios used for determining ceiling height, the placement of doors, and other architectural features. ▪ The idea that mathematical concepts have special meanings has generated a fascinating school of thought known as spiritual geometry. Some anthropologists, psychologists, and mathematicians say that certain shapes like the circle and the hexagon will influence our minds and emotions, helping us feel calm and centered. Practitioners of Eastern philosophies like *feng shui* and *vástu shástra* may combine an understanding of mathematical ratios with an awareness of energy patterns. Artists and designers frequently imbue their work with geometric symbols because they know we are shaped by the shapes around us.

opposite *This graceful chair has a slightly trapezoidal shape, suggesting strength and stability. The long, straight lines of the tall, multipaned window add to the sense of order and calm.*

You need not be mathematically gifted to draw wisdom from geometric principles. The patterns are already inside you, so you may find yourself subconsciously drawn to the most satisfying room arrangements. Play with the rhythmic repetition of designs and textures and notice how they affect the atmosphere of the room. Repeated stripes will suggest energy and excitement, while the echo of curving lines will promote a sense of calm. Look for balance and symmetry, remembering that the human form is not, itself, perfectly balanced. Try introducing an unexpected shape; don't be afraid to depart from the predictable. You will find comfort in order, but you may also find peace and joy in quirky details that express your individuality.

Lines and Shapes

If you could imagine your home without color or texture, seeing only the contours of furnishings, walls, windows, and ceilings, then you would discover a web of intersecting lines forming squares and triangles, circles and oblongs, and a variety of more complex shapes. Like Chinese calligraphy, these lines embody meanings and express emotions that may be soothing or energizing, reassuring or disturbing. They are unchanging archetypes found everywhere in the universe, from the spiral of distant galaxies to the double helix of your own genetic code.

According to Zen Buddhist beliefs, the straight line suggests supreme serenity. It is like a pond with no ripples or a single, long-sustained note. However, a perfectly straight line is not likely to occur in the natural world; it is a product of human strength and ingenuity. Straight lines may be perceived as forceful and stabilizing. Columns supporting a doorway or beams across the ceiling suggest power and quickly draw our attention. At the same time, there is a sense of tension in lines that are perfectly straight. They are like taut strings, always reminding us of forces at play. This is especially true when the lines are diagonal rather than parallel. The sharp diagonals of jutting corners can suggest conflict and discord—it's no wonder that *feng shui* advises softening angular areas with round-leafed plants.

For numerologists, shapes take on special meanings according to the numbers they suggest. The triangle, for example, is widely revered because three lines are used in its creation. Across time and cultures, the number three permeates religion and legends, from the Three Graces of ancient Greece and Rome, to the Brahma-Vishnu-Shiva of Hinduism, to the Christian holy trinity. Even more powerful is the complex hexagram form made from two triangles intertwined. With six points around a center that approximates a circle, this star formation is an ancient symbol of peace and protection and also the sacred symbol of Judaism. The interlinked triangles are often said to represent the union of opposite energies: fire and water, male and female, spirit and matter, creation and destruction, *yin* and *yang*.

When choosing room arrangements, consider the mystical powers associated with the triangle, the hexagram, and the numbers they represent. Groupings of three chairs or six photographs are inherently reassuring. Placing nine books on a shelf—instead of eight or ten—may bring an inexplicable tranquility. Numerologists would say that even the dimensions we are scarcely aware of, such as the length of tables or the height of shelves, will be more calming if they are in multiples of three. It's as though the number is encoded in our psyches, reminding us that we live in a safe and orderly universe.

above *Repeated lines and shapes take on an almost hypnotic effect when rendered in black and white.*

"Be really whole and all things will come to you."

Lau-Tzu (604–531 B.C.), Chinese spiritual leader

Circles and Curves

Many cultures view the circle as the most perfect form. Symbolizing life's endless cycle, this is the shape of the ancient medicine wheels, the mystical *yin yang* symbol, and the timeless mandala. According to *feng shui* belief, an unbroken circle evokes high energy, *yang*, because the shape is compact. However, the Zen Buddhist *enso*, a free-form circle made with a single brushstroke, is considered more *yin*. Curved lines and relaxed *enso* shapes are inherently soothing. Our eyes tend to linger over the gentle arch of a cushioned chair or the imperfect form of hand-molded pottery. Some of the most comforting dwellings are womblike homes crafted by early peoples. Although they lacked conveniences we have grown to expect, igloos, adobe homes, and other elegantly simple shelters satisfied a deep need for soft, rounded forms.

Expressing wholeness, unity, and timelessness, circular forms are both powerful and reassuring. They reflect the Sun and Moon, the curve of the Earth, and the cycle of life and the seasons. Symbols that incorporate the circle often take on mystical significance, bringing comfort, healing, and inspiration. Incorporating circular shapes into the design of your rooms is a meaningful way to invite tranquility. Arrange furnishings into these formations, or seek these patterns in fabrics and wallcoverings. Display artwork with circle motifs, or bring inside water-smoothed stones and other samples of nature's rounded shapes.

"Imagine a hoop so large that everything is in it—all two-leggeds like us, four-leggeds, the fishes of the streams, the wings of the air, and all green things that grow. Everything is together in this great hoop."

Black Elk (1863–1950), medicine man of the Oglala Sioux Indians, as told to U.S. author John Neihardt

opposite The circle is your passage to serenity, according to mystical beliefs. In this innovative corridor, a rounded doorway frames the angular lines of a translucent screen.

serenity secret #13

Cast a circle of safety. Plant both feet firmly on the ground and feel the energy of the earth below and the sky above. Visualize this energy as warm, golden honey that will strengthen and protect you. Reach down and cup the earth energy in one hand. Reach up and gather the sky energy in your other hand. Then face your palms outward and turn a slow circle. Reach high and low to form a transparent but impenetrable sphere of energy all around you. When you sense that your safety circle is set, close your eyes and savor the feelings of comfort and security.

Soothing Circles

Mandala: In the Sanskrit language, the word *mandala* means circle, both the circumference and everything contained inside. Since ancient times, cultures around the world have used images inside a circular frame as a vehicle for spiritual transformation. Every mandala is as unique as a snowflake, expressing the inner life of the person who created it.

Yin Yang: Also known as the tai chi symbol, the ancient Chinese *yin yang* design expresses the perfect balance of opposing energies. The light and dark teardrop shapes seem to spin inside the circular frame. *Yin* is the female, passive, night energy, while *Yang* is the male, active, daylight energy. Contemplating the *yin yang* symbol is a way of affirming the harmony of the universe.

Spoked Wheel: Across time and cultures, circular shapes with radiating spokes or petals are important symbols of nature's cycles. They are found in Egyptian hieroglyphics, early Chinese ideography, Nordic folk art, and Native American icons. Contemplating the spoked wheel is a way of preparing for life's important passages.

above & opposite *Circles are the most pleasing form, according to ancient wisdoms. Use round shapes to soften corners and ease cold, linear spaces.*

🌳 | **serenity secret #14**

Draw a mandala. The powerful symbol of life has brought comfort and inspiration since ancient times. Begin by drawing a circle on paper or canvas. Spontaneously draw or doodle inside the circle, creating any patterns or images that come to mind. Work without thought or plan, choosing colors or shapes as they rise to the surface of your consciousness. When your mandala is complete, you will have an evocative image of your inner self. Spend a few moments each day viewing the design and reflecting on the intricate beauty of your soul.

Triad: Three small circles nested side by side within a large circle is an almost universal symbol for unity of mind, body, and spirit. The triad, or trinity, icon is found in the art of many cultures from Tibet to ancient Europe.

Spiral: The endless swirl of an incomplete circle has symbolic meaning in many cultures, from the Celts of Great Britain to the Australian Aborigines. The design usually signifies the eternal cycle of birth, death, and rebirth.

Labyrinth: Symbolizing life's journey, the labyrinth is a meandering pathway of circles and spirals derived from the archetypal patterns of nature. When we draw a labyrinth or walk through a labyrinth garden, we travel to our own center and then return to the conscious world, enlightened and refreshed.

Enso: This empty, sweeping circle, formed by a single, relaxed brushstroke, lies at the heart of Zen Buddhist beliefs. The circumference of the circle represents the endless cycles of the material world. The emptiness in the center symbolizes the absence of mind that comes with *satori*, or the Zen state of enlightenment.

Pattern and Texture

We often think of serene places as having a smooth, uniform color. Certainly a room will not feel restful if there is an explosion of surface detailing clamoring for attention. Bold plaids, bright stripes, flashy florals, and colorful swirls create an energy that is difficult to ignore.

However, it would not be possible—or desirable—to create a room entirely devoid of pattern and texture. After all, nature itself is abundantly patterned. The delicate swirls inside a seashell, the intricate webbing of a leaf, and the exquisite speckles of color on a single stone fascinate and excite without disturbing. In the same way, you can use surface detailing to introduce depth and drama without creating discord.

Used judiciously, well-chosen prints and textures bring rhythm and movement to an otherwise uninviting room. Very small patterns create the illusion of texture, seeming almost solid from a distance. Gentle variations in colors and texture help soften kitchens, offices, and entertainment areas where appliances and machinery dominate. Simple symmetrical patterns suggest order and stability.

Because straight lines can evoke tension, striped ticking, checked gingham, and other linear patterns are best used in moderation. To soften the effect of stripes and plaids, choose muted tones and alternate patterned areas with solid blocks of color. Place the plaid pillow on an unpatterned sofa and use striped wallpaper on only one wall or on the upper or lower portion of the walls.

Patterns that feature curved flowing lines mimic forms we find in nature. Chintz fabrics with softly colored floral patterns suggest peaceful garden views. Wallpaper and stenciling with leaf-and-vine patterns help blur the boundaries between indoors and out. Special paint effects that involve sponging and stippling mimic the subtle variations we find in stone, leather, or wood. The three-dimensional character of rough plaster, brick, or stucco finishes is invitingly tactile. These natural textures take on added richness when applied with subtlety, using neutral colors.

above *Rich, earthy colors unify the patterns in a tiled kitchen wall. The curved lines of the border soften the angular diamond design.*

🌳 **serenity secret #15**

Create a Zen sand garden. For centuries, Buddhist monks have found serenity by contemplating the lines and textures of sand and stones. Although many Zen gardens are room sized, you can design one small enough to set on a tabletop. Simply fill a deep tray or baking pan with crushed granite followed by a thick layer of smooth, white sand. If you choose, you may also add a few stones or a miniature Buddha figure. Use a fork or a comb to create patterns in the sand and set aside time in your busy day to meditate on the swirling shapes and lines. When you are ready to invite change into your life, rake in new designs.

"Rhythm is our universal mother tongue.
It's the language of the soul."

Gabrielle Roth, contemporary U.S. musician,
philosopher, and dancer

above *Rhythm comes from the measured repetition of shapes and colors. In an all-white room, carefully placed splashes of color add excitement and also create a soothing sense of rhythm and order.*

Rhythm and Repetition

Before birth, every infant feels the steady beat of its mother's heart and, unconsciously, we all sense the rhythm of our own hearts. In design, the measured repetition of similar lines, shapes, patterns, colors, and textures creates a sense of rhythm that calms and reassures. Indeed, a room composed of disjointed, unrelated details without any sense of ordered repetition is certain to feel cluttered and chaotic.

To assure that the rhythms in your home are calming, limit yourself to a few key elements. Repeat a single color from your carpeting in a pillow, a lampshade, and a painting. Or, choose fabrics that echo variations of the wallpaper pattern. Use a single color to unify contrasting patterns and a matching pattern to unify contrasting colors. Let the rhythm come from the repetition of like things. Display collections according to color, shape and theme. Group wooden duck carvings on the mantel or hang antique tools on one wall. Also find rhythm in shapes and lines. Combine straight, linear chairs with family photographs in square frames. In a room with rounded arches, use repeated floral motifs.

While continuity is needed to establish a satisfying rhythm, too much sameness can create a room that is merely boring. Don't be afraid to introduce variation in the repeated elements. Echo several different tones from the same color family and repeat smaller or larger versions of a dominant pattern. The rhythm will be effective so long as there is a single dominant theme to unify the room.

Soothing Design

- *Soft curves*
- *Rounded forms*
- *Archetypal patterns*
- *Nature-inspired textures*
- *Repeated shapes and colors*
- *Symmetrical arrangements*
- *Balanced proportions*

"You must learn to be still in the midst of activity and to be vibrantly alive in repose."

Indira Gandhi (1917–1984), Indian political leader

opposite *Balanced arrangements need not be perfectly symmetrical. Here, the pillow on one chair balances the painting on the opposite wall.*

Balance and Symmetry

We often use the words *centered* or *balanced* to describe how we feel when we are at peace with ourselves. The need for equilibrium is both physical and psychological: We must keep balance to walk upright and our emotions must maintain balance for us to function in our work and our relationships.

A room that is centered has a focal point or center of attention. A painting, an unusual furnishing, or an architectural feature serves as the center of attention. Balanced arrangements of shapes, colors, or patterns draw our gaze in a smooth arch around the room. Without the focal point, our attention wanders aimlessly, and without balance, we are likely to feel lopsided and insecure.

The focal point usually is not literally in the center of the space. Chances are, you would quickly tire of a perfectly symmetrical room with matching furniture arranged like mirror reflections. Instead, dissimilar objects may be balanced according to their substance, weight, or psychological powers. Two chairs beneath a window help balance a single heavy bed at the far side of the room; a grouping of sofas and chairs balances the imposing piano in the alcove; an arrangement of small photographs balances a larger portrait on the opposite wall. Balance also refers to the placement of color, pattern, and texture. A burgundy vase on the mantle balances the deep red carpet on the hearth; sheer billowy curtains balance soft cotton bed linens; floral motifs stenciled along the ceiling balance hanging pots of trailing ivy.

Scale and Proportion

Beauty has no size. A delicate Chippendale chair and a heavy oak banquet table have the same potential to inspire delight. Yet, we feel ill at ease the moment these two items are paired. Similarly, we may feel oppressed or overwhelmed by large, sweeping patterns in a small, confined space or a ponderous wardrobe in a tiny bedchamber. Items that are out of proportion quickly arouse anxiety and we usually don't want to be near them.

We feel the most relaxed in rooms where furnishings and details are well proportioned in relationship to each other and also to the persons who will be using them. Small children see the world from a different perspective than adults; they may feel comforted in rooms you would find claustrophobic. In contrast, a grown man is likely to feel most at ease when surrounded by objects that have heft and substance.

Contemporary homes often include expansive open spaces where family and friends gather, play games, and watch television or listen to music. The space may flow without boundaries into the dining area and kitchen, forming a single, large great room. Ultramodern loft-style homes may even place sleeping areas in the center of a vast open space.

These grand spaces impress and inspire, but they are not necessarily reassuring. Soaring cathedral ceilings can feel profoundly spiritual, or they can leave individuals feeling diminished and vulnerable. The most restful homes strike a balance between expansive open spaces and small, protected areas. To create comfort and intimacy in open areas, use color and lighting to delineate the space. By painting the walls a slightly lighter or darker tone, you establish a subtle boundary and help reduce the overwhelming size of the space. Use small table lamps with warm, incandescent bulbs to define areas with cozy pools of light. Carpets can also be very effective in establishing the sense of a room within a room.

left *Plants with large, rounded leaves will release the tension of sharp, angular lines.*

opposite *A well-planned seating arrangement with a careful balance of shapes, lines, colors, and textures will set the scene for peaceful meals. In some traditions, the number three is considered sacred.*

Unity and Harmony

Carefully composed, harmonious rooms are deeply relaxing. We feel centered because objects are arranged with sensitivity for scale, proportion, and balance. The thoughtful placement of shapes and the measured repetition of colors and patterns help unify the space, creating a "look" or ambiance.

You need not limit yourself to matching furniture or coordinated patterns to create harmony. Strong color accents echoed in fabric designs and artwork can unify even the most startling combinations. A consistent use of shapes, patterns, or textures will also bind together elements that, on first glance, do not appear to match.

Dare to place a primitive wood carving on a mahogany sideboard. Try mingling crystal with clay, chrome with oak, silk with sisal. Unexpected partnerships will work as long as there is a connecting theme. The tie that binds can be a specific style such as French Country or Art Moderne, but more frequently the sense of unity will come from the personalities of the people using the space. Choose furnishings and objects you truly love and you may be surprised at how well they harmonize. Incorporate details that express the differing—and even conflicting—tastes and interests of your family. Finding harmony and order in the midst of differences is a potent way to reinforce family stability.

opposite *Unexpected combinations of colors and textures entice the sense of touch. Here, timeworn stones against the grain of natural oak create a soothing counterpoint to cool metallic chairs.*

"All that is harmony for thee, O Universe, is in harmony with me as well."

Marcus Aurelius (A.D. 121–180), Roman emperor

Chapter Five

Color and Light

"Colors . . . follow the changes of the emotions."

Pablo Picasso (1881–1973), Spanish artist

One of the most important things you can do to reduce the level of stress in your home is to choose calming colors that speak to your spirit. From creamy neutral tones to deep indigo, colors act as subtle yet powerful drugs, affecting both body and mind. ▪ In ancient times, physicians in China, India, and Egypt practiced *chromotherapy,* the science of stimulating physical and mental energies through color. Today, some therapists use colored lights to treat a wide range of ailments. Designers now pay close attention to the impact of color when they create interiors for hospitals, schools, stores, and restaurants. ▪ Indeed, color is so powerful that its influence is felt even when we are sleeping. Everyone, including those without sight, senses color because it is actually composed of vibrating light waves. Perceived through the skin as well as the eyes, these waves stir physiological responses that are instinctive and universal. Warm tones like yellow, orange, and red act as stimulants. They increase our pulse and respiration and may produce either excitement or anxiety. Cool colors such as blue and green are calming. They decrease our pulse and respiration and may encourage relaxation.

---

serenity secret #18

Contemplate a color. Visualize a shade that represents qualities you need in your life today. Close your eyes and breathe deeply. Imagine your chosen color filling your lungs and feel it flowing into your arms and legs. Hold the color inside and accept its power to comfort and heal. Exhale slowly, letting the color swirl around your head. Then, once again, breathe deeply, inhaling your chosen color.

opposite *Blue, yellow, and green are a playful but harmonious mix in an informal dining area. The napkins, china, and flowers echo the cheerful scheme and help balance the colors.*

Color Tips

- Seek colors that express qualities that your family values.

- Use color to bring out qualities you would like to encourage.

- Take cues from the surrounding landscape.

- Look for colors in woodwork and other structural elements of your home.

- Find colors that enhance your own skin tones.

- Experiment with lighter and darker shades of the same color.

- Consider the impact of lighting and surrounding objects on the colors you see.

- Remember the ceilings: Think beyond basic white.

- Forget trends; choose colors that are most reassuring and uplifting for you and your family.

However, there is no easy formula for choosing colors. Although they arouse the same physiological responses in all of us, we are likely to react quite differently emotionally. Many of our color associations come from cultural beliefs and traditions. For example, in China, red suggests happiness, while Westerners often associate the color with rage. In turn, the color red may be imbued with layers of meaning based on childhood memories of a favorite toy or an upsetting incident. Ethnic or national associations will also affect our responses. During times of war, colors from our national flag will carry greater emotional resonance.

Finding the colors that comfort and reassure you and your family will require some soul searching and a bit of experimentation. Pay close attention to the choices family members make in their clothing and other personal items. Reflect on the colors most often found at favorite vacation spots. Talk about fond childhood memories and the colors they invoke.

Seeking the Comforting Colors

You may discover that each member of the household has a somewhat different preference for color. Encourage personal choices for private areas such as bedrooms, but also look for a single color that best represents the needs and values of the family as a whole. Gather samples from several venues—paint stores, fabric centers, flower shops, and your own closet. Scatter swatches and samples about the house; spend several weeks studying the colors and narrowing your selections. Paint a single wall and observe how your chosen color feels in the changing light. Also pay close attention to the behavior of children; although they are not always able to articulate their feelings, they may become more anxious or irritable in the presence of some colors.

Once you have discovered the most comforting color for you and your family, use it as a theme throughout your entire home. In some rooms, walls or ceilings may be painted in your chosen family color; in other rooms, the color may be echoed in a carpet, a painting, or a vase of flowers. Choose a slightly darker or lighter shade for a wallpaper boarder or an upholstered chair. The smooth flow of colors through your home will symbolically represent family unity and will enhance the aura of safety and protection.

Sky Colors

Suggesting sky and sea, heaven and the universe, blue is an ethereal, holy hue. From whisper-soft powder blue to deep cobalt, this magical color has the power to calm troubled children, diminish aggression, and ease many symptoms of stress. Linger in a room where blue is dominant and you will soon fall under its spell. Your blood pressure will lower and you will breathe more slowly. In this relaxed state, you may feel more in tune with your spirituality. Quiet meditation will come more easily in a pale blue room. Darker hues will enhance concentration and the ability to work productively.

A room need not be all blue to reap the benefits of this healing color. In fact, too much blue is likely to feel cool and impersonal. Because it is tranquilizing, blue can act as a mild depressant. To create rooms that are both restful and welcoming, consider combining blues with warm, earthy colors.

above Soft powder blues blend beautifully with light, natural colors. These gentle hues promote relaxed conversation, while the minute splashes of orange energize the space.

opposite Cool blue surfaces recede from our eyes and tend to make rooms appear larger. Combined with white, blues are deeply restful and inspire quiet contemplation.

Blue

- *Relaxes the nervous system.*

- *Encourages quiet contemplation.*

- *Enhances concentration.*

- *May evoke melancholy.*

- *May suppress the appetite.*

- *Lighter shades help promote conversation.*

- *Darker shades suggest confidence and dependability.*

A touch of deep rose or lemon yellow will bring warmth to dusty blues. Burgundy or burnt sienna will add an air of comfort to strong, assertive blues such as navy and cobalt.

Like a tropical ocean, blue has many depths and infinite variations. While most are calm and appealing, not all are equally serene. Periwinkle takes on a purple hue that can be either tranquilizing or troubling. While lavender is often associated with romance or spirituality, it is a restless, uncertain color. According to some findings, colors that combine blue and red may actually trigger stress because our eyes have difficulty registering the two frequencies together. For a more restful atmosphere, mingle lavender, violet, and purples with more pure shades of blue.

Some of the most serene landscapes in the world are found on tiny Greek islands scattered across the Mediterranean Sea. Brilliant blue detailing on stark white buildings echo the sea and sky, creating the illusion that doors and windows open into a wondrous, deeply spiritual space. If you have a bright, sunlit room, you can create the same mystical aura by combining crisp white with a single, unwavering shade of blue.

"Green comes from blue, but it surpasses blue."

Chinese proverb

Tree Colors

In nearly every part of the world, trees represent growth and renewal. Their leaves—ranging from brilliant emerald to dusky olive—perform a miraculous alchemy, synthesizing sunlight into sustenance. It's no wonder that greens are so often chosen for hospital walls; these restful, nature-inspired tones ease pain, lessen anxiety, combat depression, and promote a general sense of well-being.

Despite its many variations, green is uncomplicated. It harmonizes easily with other colors and also with itself. Furnishings and accents in various shades of green often can be mixed and matched or carried off to different parts of the house. Unlike blue, which will seem melancholy if used to excess, green does not wear out its welcome. Feel free to fill an entire room with this soothing color. Instead of overwhelming, the abundance of green will suggest the stillness of a deep forest. Take your cues from nature when choosing accents. Combine olive green with natural wood and ruddy browns; seafoam green with sand and coral; fruity greens with bright blossom colors like pink, red, and gold. If you can mimic the colors outside your window, the simple joys of nature will follow you inside, bringing a deep sense of belonging and a promise of new beginnings.

Green

- *Restful for the eyes.*
- *Promotes relaxation.*
- *Eases pain.*
- *Suggests health, growth, and renewal.*
- *Considered sacred in the Muslim faith.*
- *Implies wealth in the United States.*

🌳 | **serenity secret #19**

Sip green tea. Choose an elegant cup without a handle and practice an ancient Japanese *chado* ceremony. Originated by Buddhist monks, the ritual of brewing and serving tea is a way of disciplining the mind and preparing for meditation. It takes many years of study to be a tea master, but you can begin by savoring the flavor and aroma of the warm, soothing beverage. You'll also enjoy health benefits: Ingredients in green tea help control blood pressure and slow the aging process.

above *Serene greens come in many shades, from shadowy grays to the cheery yellow-green of budding leaves. Choose deeper tones for relaxation; move toward the bright spring greens for active work and play areas.*

above With walls painted a mossy green, this informal bedroom captures the outdoors. The white-trimmed doorway and windows offer dazzling views of gleaming woodwork and the woods beyond.

"Nature's first green is gold,"

Robert Frost (1874–1963), U.S. poet

Brown

- *Affirms ties to the natural world.*
- *Suggests stability, strength, and maturity.*
- *Helps calm anxiety.*
- *Harmonizes easily with other colors.*
- *Represents masculinity in Western cultures.*

Gold

- *Stimulates the immune system.*
- *Eases depression.*
- *Boosts the libido.*
- *Suggests wealth and luxury.*

Earth Colors

Colors drawn from the earth are comforting because they affirm our connection with nature. Earth-inspired colors like buff, straw, khaki, burnt umber, burnt sienna, taupe, and stone may also feel more authentic than bright, jelly bean colors. In home offices, entertainment rooms, or kitchens, nature's palette will help soften the effect of machinery and electronics.

Subtle, earth-hewn colors are far from bland. Deep browns, suggesting confidence and rootedness, become warm and passionate when they are tinged with red or orange. Nearly brown moss and khaki take on many of the tension-taming qualities of more vivid greens. Rocky grays can evoke the spirituality and serenity of brighter whites. Metallics—gold, bronze, copper, and silver—suggest both solidity and abundance; they bring a sense of luxury to even the most rustic interiors.

The ever-shifting hues of desert sands and canyon walls are wonderfully harmonious. Brown, beige, olive, and gray will blend together in your home as beautifully as they do in nature. Even the more intense shades—bordering on crimson—bring excitement without discord.

opposite *From dusty tans to olive greens, nature's earthy colors mix easily and suggest a comfortable connection to the land.*

Fire Colors

Suggesting flickering flames, red, yellow, orange, and magenta demand our attention. We call these colors "warm" or "hot" because they arouse our passions. Regardless of the personal or cultural meanings we assign them, they act as stimulants, increasing pulse and respiration. Fire colors may cause agitation and heighten anxiety, yet, when contained, they can bring a warmth that is as comforting as candlelight.

Moderation is the key. A splash of scarlet in the dining room will stimulate the appetite, but too much red is likely to aggravate family squabbles. A touch of daffodil in the home office can boost your energy and productivity, but an overabundance will disrupt your ability to concentrate.

To enjoy fire colors in serene environments, consider using toned down versions. Colors like burgundy, deep gold, and rust combine the warmth of fire with the stabilizing forces of brown and other earth colors. For more intensity, bring in a pot of blooming sunflowers or combine bright details with pastels and soft neutrals.

above *Reds and yellows capture the passion and warmth of a flickering fire. Used in a busy activity area, they will heighten the senses and stimulate conversation.*

Red

- *Stimulates the nervous system.*
- *Heightens the senses.*
- *Increases energy.*
- *Promotes feelings of power.*
- *May heighten feelings of anger and hostility.*
- *Can be balanced by combining with green.*

Yellow

- *Stimulates the mind and heightens awareness.*
- *Helps lift depression.*
- *Boosts memory and perception.*
- *May heighten anxiety.*
- *Can be balanced by combining with blue.*

Orange

- *Stimulates emotional responses.*
- *Eases depression.*
- *Promotes sociability.*
- *Heightens creativity.*
- *May aggravate nervous tension.*
- *Can be balanced by combining with green-blues colors.*

Pink

- *Suppresses anger and hostility.*
- *Suppresses the appetite.*
- *Suggests tenderness and romance.*
- *May cause fatigue.*
- *Represents femininity in Western cultures.*
- *Ideal for sleeping areas.*

🌳 | **serenity secret #20**

Drape a sheer pink scarf over the shade of your bedside lamp. Studies show that pale, rosy hues have a tranquilizing effect. The soothing glow will surround you completely, transporting you back to a time before birth.

---

above *Fuchsia is a hot, almost-red pink, yet its effect can be sedating, especially when surrounded by calming blues and grays.*

right *You may not want to fill an entire room with potent, deeply tranquilizing pink. Instead, bring in a vase of fragrant, rosy blooms.*

Womb Colors

Combining the purity and spirituality of white with the passion of red, pink speaks to our subconscious, evoking the sense of safety we must have felt in our mothers' wombs. According to psychologists, prisoners exhibit less aggression when their cells are painted a deep shade of pink. Indeed, most people will find it difficult to behave aggressively when surrounded by this tranquilizing color.

We rarely think of using pink as the dominant color for primary living areas, perhaps because it is so very effective. While it relaxes the muscles and eases tension, pink can actually sap your energy. Bright pink is also an appetite suppressant, making it a poor choice for cooking and dining areas—unless your goal is to minimize stress-related snacking.

The most calming pinks are, surprisingly, the most intense. Vivid watermelon colors may leave you feeling drowsy, while softer powder pinks will soothe without sedating. Earthy adobe and sand tones provide a more subtle comfort and harmonize well with other colors. For just a whiff of pink, borrow iridescent, nearly white colors from seashells and pearls.

"The eye doesn't see any shapes, it sees only what is differentiated through light and dark or through colors."

Johann Wolfgang von Goethe (1749–1832), German poet and dramatist

White

- *Embodies all colors.*
- *Suggests spirituality.*
- *Encourages meditation.*
- *Awakens creativity.*
- *Amplifies the effect of other colors.*
- *Embraces the pure bright light of the Sun.*

Black

- *Suggests safety and protection.*
- *Calms anxieties.*
- *Represents spirituality in Eastern cultures.*
- *Represents death in Western cultures.*
- *Helps balance the energies of other colors.*

above *An all-white room can be highly sensual, calling our attention to the subtle interplay of light and shadow.*

Snow Colors

Often perceived as the absence of color, white encompasses the entire spectrum. It is the quizzical combination of color and noncolor, being and nothingness. In some cultures, white connotes death; it is used for funerals and mourning. In other cultures, white suggests purity and innocence; it is used for weddings and important religious ceremonies such as baptisms and christenings. Almost universally, white is considered profoundly spiritual, representing the perfect bright light of natural sunshine—and of heaven.

The whites seen in our daily lives are not, in fact, as pure as sunlight. They are the slightly gray color of chalk or the yellowed color of heavy cream or the pinkish hue of pearls. Even the brilliant white of modern paints, which does not yellow with age, has a bluish cast. White is also reflective; it will take its tints from other objects in the room. The rosy colors in a floral wallpaper, the lush greens of a flourishing ficus plant, or the yellow glow of incandescent lighting will transform the appearance of surfaces painted white. Because the color is so adaptable and because distractions are minimized, rooms where white predominates can be deeply restful. An all-white room becomes rather like a Zen sand garden, an

below *Don't rule out black and nearly black shades of gray. Combined with white, darker colors suggest safety and comfort. Here, wood-carvings over the headboard reflect continuity and a sense of personal history.*

exquisitely still space that encourages meditation. Our attention is drawn to lines, shapes, and subtle variations in textures. We begin to relax as we contemplate the interplay of light and shadow and the enticing whispers of colors that seem to hover just below the surface.

Night Colors

As day turns into night, the absence of light brings another absence of color: black. In some parts of the world, black represents the noncolor that is the sum of all colors. Through this darkness, one may enter the spiritual realm. A mostly black room will feel restful and secure if it includes details that carry warm emotional resonance, such as photographs of family members or treasured works of art. Black accents in an all-white room can have a soothing, almost hypnotic effect. Together, black and white express spiritual unity, suggesting *yin* and *yang*, heaven and earth, body and soul.

Light and Shadow

The movement of the Sun makes chameleons of our homes. A wall that you thought you had painted seafoam green may appear blue at dawn, gray at dusk, and lime in the tungsten glow of a reading lamp. The changing light will also cast shape-shifting shadows as it filters through curtains or blinds. With each transformation in color or pattern, the emotional tenor of the room also changes.

The lighting you choose will have an enormous impact on your physical and emotional well-being. We all need a certain amount of natural sunlight in order to feel healthy and emotionally balanced. The ultraviolet radiation generated by the Sun affects our levels of serotonin, a hormone that influences our brain activities and affects our emotions. Humans deprived of ultraviolet light are likely to feel melancholy and lethargic, and may develop a form of clinical depression known as seasonal affective disorder (SAD).

To create environments that will help you maintain emotional equilibrium, try to capitalize on the amount of sunlight that enters your home. You don't necessarily need large windows; instead, make note of the Sun's direction and place furnishings so that you will benefit from the afternoon light.

Avoid bulky, light-blocking window treatments. Venetian blinds or sheer curtains will filter the light without darkening the room. Or, for soft sunlight and inhibited views, consider using specialized window glazings. Nearly transparent films applied to your existing glass will filter out glare and provide the privacy you need.

Artificial lighting is very different from the light generated by the Sun. Standard incandescent bulbs produce a reddish glow, while traditional fluorescent bulbs usually produce light with a yellow-green cast. Incandescent bulbs made with neodymium glass will cast a glow that appears very similar to natural sunlight. Full-spectrum fluorescent bulbs emit all the Sun's frequencies, including a small, safe level of ultraviolet radiation.

"Colors seen by candle-light
Will not look the same by day."

Elizabeth Barrett Browning (1806–1861), British poet

🌳 serenity secret #21

Light a candle and gaze steadily into the flame. Concentrating on a single object is a form of meditation. As you watch the flickering light, your pulse will slow, your blood pressure will lower, and your adrenaline levels will drop. After five or ten minutes, blow out the candle with a long, slow sigh.

above *Colors will change their hue in the golden glow of incandescent bulbs. Experiment with a variety of light sources to find the most pleasing effect.*

To create the most pleasing and most soothing effect, you will want to experiment with a variety of different lamps and different wattages. The most beneficial lighting is uniform in brightness. Very bright light—whether it comes from the Sun or an artificial source—is likely to create high contrast, leading to eyestrain and headaches. For living areas, you may prefer the warm ruddy glow of incandescent lamps, while in work areas, you may opt for cool, diffused full-spectrum lighting. When all you need is soft, atmospheric illumination, don't forget the romantic glow of the Moon and the warm, comforting flicker of candlelight.

Chapter Six

Sound, Scent, and Texture

"Our dreams drench us in senses, and senses steep us again in dreams."

Amos Bronson Alcott (1799–1888), U.S. teacher, philosopher, reformer

Tranquil spaces are wonderfully sensual. Subtle variations in texture tempt our fingers to linger over the things we touch. In the stillness we hear wind or water or haunting music that echoes the rhythms of our bodies. Barely perceptible aromas evoke poignant memories and blanket us with serenity. Even our sense of taste is tantalized by bright berry colors or inviting fragrances. ▪ Time stops when we look beyond the things we can see and focus on hearing, smelling, tasting, and touch. As the senses heighten, worries over the future and remorse over the past diminish. Surrounding ourselves with things we love and paying close attention to their sensual pleasures is a form of meditation, ever reminding us to live in the moment. ▪ Often, the most pleasing sensations are the subtlest. Serene spaces do not shout for attention; instead, the details entice, intrigue, and invite in ways that are seductive and far reaching. In Eastern mystical thought, the ideal is to move beyond sensory distractions and to discover a quiet, empty space—*prajna* in Sanskrit—of pure energy and spirit. Focusing on a single, well-chosen sensory detail is a way toward that stillness. ▪ Elevate your awareness with quiet sounds or just a hint of fragrance. Accentuate textures by using neutral monochrome color schemes and, when illumination is not needed, try turning out the lights and exploring the beauty of your home through the tips of your fingers. According to the ancient beliefs, you achieve peace when you become one with the things you sense.

🌳 | serenity secret #22

Soak away your stress. Sprinkle your bathwater with fragrant rosemary oil and use a rough loofah or a brush to scrub toxins from your skin. Savor the sensations of warmth and wetness, rough and soapy smooth. Listen closely to the splashing of the water and your own breathing. Focusing on your senses will ease your nerves, and you will feel soothed and comforted by your own caring touch.

opposite *Water and sunlight are the two key ingredients for easing life's stresses. A deep pedestal tub beside a tall window allows bathers to savor both. The golden glow of natural woodwork adds to the tranquil atmosphere.*

Sound

The air is never still. Every movement of every object sends out the vibrations we perceive as sounds. There is no pause in the hums, buzzes, thunks, clicks, rattles, rings, squeals, and squeaks that surround us, and each noise, no matter how small, alters the vibrations in our own bodies, affecting how we think and feel.

Some of the most soothing sounds come from nature. Surely there is nothing more peaceful than the rustle of leaves, the patter or rain, or the chirp and chatter of birds. The rhythmic swish of cascading waves is nearly hypnotic in soft syncopation. And, while nature is performing its medleys, your home never ceases to make its own comforting sounds. Close your eyes and you may be able to hear the hum of the refrigerator, the whir of a fan, or the creak of a wooden floor. Pausing to focus your attention on these sounds will help ease worries and relieve symptoms of stress.

Music—both vocal and instrumental—truly is food for the soul. We are ourselves rhythmic creatures and certain types of music help us tune into the metronome beat of our hearts. Many cultures incorporate chanting, drumming, and other rhythmic activities into their spiritual practice. In India, the ancient teachings of Grandharva Ved aspire to harmonize human life through the artful use of sound and vibration. The melodies and rhythms of Grandharva Ved are said to relieve ailments, integrate body and soul, and evoke a state of pure bliss.

Today, music is widely used in hospitals and treatment centers to ease pain and relieve fear, anxiety, and depression. In addition to listening to carefully selected music, patients sing, chant, play instruments, and create their own compositions. No musical talent or experience is necessary to enjoy the healing power of therapeutic sound; we all respond instinctively to rhythm and melody. You can enjoy these benefits in your own home simply by surrounding yourself with sounds that soothe you.

Begin by banishing harsh, discordant noise. Honking horns, ringing telephones, rumbling machinery, loud clangs, and booming stereos are not merely unpleasant—they rattle your nerves, deplete your energy, and can actually make you sick. To still the noise, soundproof your windows with insulated curtains, or install double-paned windows.

"The human being is essentially sound, vibrations, and melody . . . "

Holger Kalweit, contemporary German anthropologist and author

🌳 | **serenity secret #23**

Sing. Fill your lungs with air and sing a show tune, a popular song, or even a TV jingle. Don't worry if you are off key. The deep breathing will relieve your stress, and the music will release your inhibitions.

below *A length of woolen carpet helps define this hallway, creating a tempting view of the piano room. When doors are open, the music can easily be heard in the kitchen and living area.*

Heavy drapes, soft pillows, plush carpeting, and fabric wall hangings will absorb sounds inside your home. Even tall leafy plants can help to muffle reverberating noise.

Listening to music will do wonders to alleviate stress. Choose the style of music that seems to best match your own personality and rhythms. Also, play recordings of rainfall and other natural sounds, or, simply close your eyes and listen to the soothing rhythms of your own deep breathing.

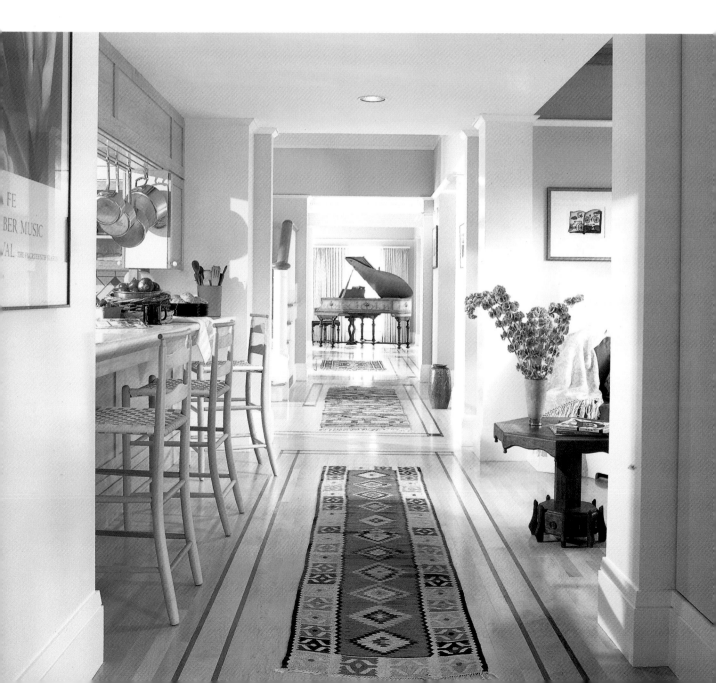

Fragrance

Aromas permeate every part of our lives. Even when we are not conscious of them, they slip into our psyche, awakening long-forgotten memories and stirring up a strong brew of emotions. The scent of favorite foods can be especially evocative; just a whiff of baking bread or brewing coffee can recall a time when we felt completely safe and nurtured. Certain floral scents like lavender and rose gardenia work like tranquilizers. When these aromas are absorbed through the ocular nerves or the skin, they help ease muscle tension and headaches.

above *The scent of roses has long been celebrated for its soothing properties. Hearty climbing roses will cascade over fences and walls, surrounding the home in fragrance. Floating candles add to the romantic atmosphere.*

right *Naturally scented soaps made with herbs and essential plant oils are free of harsh, synthetic perfumes.*

Soothing Scents

For deep relaxation, seek essential oils from these healing plants:

- *Cedar*
- *Chamomile*
- *Lavender*
- *Lemon*
- *Marjoram*
- *Orange*
- *Rose*
- *Sage*
- *Sandlewood*
- *Violet*
- *Ylang-ylang*

Capitalizing on the therapeutic value of aroma, some practitioners use essential oils from flowers, herbs, seeds, leaves, and roots to treat a variety of stress-related ailments. You can enjoy the healing power of aroma in your own home by lighting naturally scented candles or burning fragrant, all-natural incense. For the best results, make sure that your candles and incense are made with genuine plant oils and do not contain synthetic products.

Many health food stores offer the same type of pure, premium-quality essential oils that aromatherapists use. To unleash the power of these highly concentrated potions, place just a few drops of essential oil in an electric vaporizer or in a diffuser over a candle or lightbulb. Add a bit of essential oil to water and use a mister to spritz the air with soothing scents, or sprinkle the oil on a potpourri of dried pinecones, flower petals, and berries. Or, simply drop a bit of essential oil in your bathwater and give yourself permission to soak in the warm, calming fragrance.

While pleasing aromas can sooth us, unpleasant odors may actually arouse anxiety. We cannot feel completely at ease in rooms that are haunted by lingering smells from last night's meal, tobacco smoke, or harsh cleaning products. Simply opening a window may help freshen the air. If smells persist, you may want to install HEPA air filters and check your kitchen ventilation systems. Some kitchen fans are ductless; instead of removing odors to the outdoors, they recirculate the air through filters that must be periodically changed.

One of the easiest ways to assure that the fragrances in your home are fresh and appealing is to avoid using strong, ammonia-based cleaning products. Instead, choose gentle, natural cleaners like vinegar and lemon juice. Then, fill your home with the natural scents and calming beauty of fresh-cut peonies, sprigs of honeysuckle, or a pot of blooming chrysanthemums.

serenity secret #24

Practice progressive muscle relaxation (PMR). Clench your fist as tightly as you can. Relax. Then, relax even more, making your hand as loose as possible. The process of clenching and progressively relaxing will help relieve stress. Try PMR on different muscle groups or on your whole body.

right *The scent of flowers, the flavor of fresh fruit, and the softness of a beloved pet are just a few sensual pleasures evoked by this inviting space. At the far end of the room, a crackling fire offers comforting warmth and sound.*

Touch

Your skin is your largest organ, blanketing your entire body with keen sensation. The moment you enter a room, you perceive the temperature and humidity, and these perceptions alone can determine your level of comfort. The first step in creating a soothing atmosphere may be as simple as setting the thermostat or lighting a warm, inviting fire.

Every human being needs to touch and be touched, and details that appeal to tactile sensations also speak to the soul. Plush velvets, whisper soft silk, and intricate woven tapestries suggest comfort and warmth, while rough hewn wood and rugged stone are beautiful reminders of nature. All textures, from the cool sheen of window glass to the downy softness of chenille, have the power to delight, but they are the most enticing when mingled. To create rooms that nourish your spirit, place flowing gauze drapery against a rugged brick wall, set gleaming bronze candlesticks on a limestone mantel, or cluster ocean-tossed shells on a velvet throw.

above *The sensual joys of texture are enhanced when rendered in neutral colors. A wispy plant becomes an object of fascination in the midst of wicker and white cotton muslin.*

Find Harmony through *Ayurveda*

Founded thousands of years ago in India, the healing tradition of **ayurveda**
(or **ayur-ved***) offers a holistic approach to dealing with stress. According to
the ancient practices, the senses—taste, touch, and aroma—help balance
mind, body, and spirit, leading to perfect health and serenity. Practicing*
*ayurveda begins with identifying the sources of stress. Every human being
is unique, and to be effective, cures must address individual needs and
must also nourish every part of the body and spirit. Each person in the
household will respond best to different flavors, fragrances, and physical
sensations. Your own needs will also vary according to the circumstances
of the day. However, simply acknowledging the importance of the senses in
relieving the symptoms of stress is an important step in promoting serenity.*

Mental Stress

*If you spend too much time on mental tasks, you may lose your ability to
make clear decisions, think positively, and sleep well. To restore balance,
it is important to avoid stimulants. Choose warm milk and other dairy
products. Calm the mind with meditation, aromatherapy, and warm oil
massages.*

Emotional Stress

*A death, a broken relationship, or any profound sadness will create dishar-
mony. You may feel irritable or depressed. If you are able to sleep, you may
find yourself waking in the night. To restore balance, choose foods associated with the functioning of the heart: sweet, juicy fruits and foods with bit-
ter, astringent tastes. Practice daily self-massage with scented coconut oil.*

Physical Stress

*Too much exercise or overexertion at work will lead to physical fatigue
and difficulty concentrating. An overly sedentary lifestyle will also create
imbalance, causing sluggish digestion, fatigue, and depression. To restore
balance, strive for moderate exercise and enhance your diet with energizing
foods such as walnuts; almonds; coconut; sweet, juicy fruits; and a variety
of cheeses.*

"I shut my eyes in order to see."

Paul Gauguin (1848–1903), French painter

Soothing Massage

Touching and being touched are nature's way to provide comfort and healing. Over many centuries, a variety of massage techniques has evolved in Thailand, Japan, China, Sweden, Germany, and other parts of the world. Listed here are just a few powerfully soothing forms of massage. Many therapists combine several techniques and add their own unique approaches to the art of healing touch.

Acupressure

By applying firm thumb and finger pressure to key points on your body, an accupressure therapist will help restore balance in your energies.

Craniosacral Balancing

This form of massage focuses on the bones in your head. The therapist will apply a light touch and very gentle movement to your scalp.

Deep Tissue Massage

Rolfing, Trager, Hellerwork, and Feldenkrais are just a few examples of this effective massage technique. Using slow, firm pressure, the therapist will work through your muscle tension layer by layer, gradually working down to knots of tension in the deep muscles. Deep tissue massage is ideal for relieving pain from injuries such as back strain or whiplash.

Orthopedic Massage

Practiced by a medical doctor, orthopedic massage treats the underlying causes of tension. Individual muscles are massaged to stimulate circulation and release knots of tension. An orthopedic massage may also include stretching, structural balancing, and a variety of other techniques.

Reflexology

A reflexology therapist will manipulate key reflex points on your body—especially on the hands and feet—to reduce tension, increase circulation, and reestablish harmony among body functions.

Reiki

Originating in ancient Tibet, Reiki combines touching with visualization to align the chakras and stimulate organs and glands. The Reiki therapist serves as a channel for healing energy; you may notice a slightly tingling sensation during treatment.

above *The earthy textures of dried flowers, cherry woodwork, and unbleached cotton bring relaxed sensuality to a serene sleeping area.*

🌳 | **Serenity Secret #26**

Feel your face. Notice the tension in your mouth, jaws, and forehead. Imagine that your face is made of wax. Visualize the tension melting; picture your face collapsing like a candle. Let out a long, slow sigh.

Shiatsu

Theories of acupuncture, acupressure, and other massage techniques are combined in this ancient Japanese art. Shiatsu strives to balance the energy, or *chi*, that moves along well-defined pathways through your body. You may rest fully clothed on a mat during a shiatsu massage.

Sports Massage

A sports massage therapist will study the movements you use in strenuous sports activities. Vigorous stroking and pressure will treat the muscles and joints in areas where they are most needed. Sports massage may be used to promote recovery or to prevent stress injuries.

Swedish Massage

Vigorous stroking, kneading, pressing, rolling, and vibrating motions will stimulate your circulation and boost your energy. A slippery coating of oil makes these movements sensuously fluid.

Watsu

Combining the techniques of Japanese Zen shiatsu with water therapy, Watsu is a form of floating massage. Your entire body will be swished through warm water while the Watsu therapist applies pressure to your joints and muscles. You may experience a sense of buoyancy and an altered sense of time.

Taste

A room cannot literally have a taste, yet we often think in terms of food when we design our spaces. A chocolate-colored sofa in a room painted cream stirs images of a delectable confection that becomes all the more tantalizing when we add peppermint-striped window blinds. Certain colors—reds, oranges, and yellows—actually stimulate the appetite, enhancing our pleasure of food.

Aromas naturally stir thoughts of eating. The two senses—taste and smell—are so closely associated that it is sometimes difficult to tell them apart. A whiff of cinnamon conjures images of muffins or apple pie, and you may have the sense that you are actually tasting these foods. Awareness of details that evoke the illusion of taste becomes especially important when designing kitchens and dining rooms. You will want to choose colors and fragrances that appeal to the appetite and avoid elements—certain shades of blue, for example—that will make food seem less appealing. Keep in mind, however, that taste is the most primal of senses and every room in your home will carry a whisper of flavor.

> **serenity secret #27**
>
> Remember your favorite childhood food. Did you love peanut butter? Strawberry ice cream? Rice pudding? Snack on it now. The flavor of a food that once comforted you will awaken peaceful memories from your past.

Mood Foods

Thoughts of chocolate may make your spirits fly, but the sugar in candy will put you on an emotional roller coaster, doctors say. To boost your mood and ward off stress, choose a healthy, balanced diet with plenty of B vitamins. These foods are best:

- *Leafy green vegetables*
- *Bananas*
- *Fish, especially salmon, sardines, tuna, and mackerel*
- *Whole-grain cereals*
- *Oranges and orange juice*

right *Jewel-bright colors stimulate the appetite in this cheerful kitchen. Reds, yellows, and oranges are especially effective for enhancing the sense of taste.*

Chapter Seven

Health and Comfort

"To keep the body in good health is a duty . . .
Otherwise, we shall not be able to keep our mind strong and clear."
Buddha

What we call *stress* is really an inherent response, as naturally occurring as the ripples on a quiet pond or the waves of the ocean. The events that trigger our stress are not necessarily bad. A joyful occasion such as a wedding, the birth of a long-awaited child, or an important job promotion will arouse the same biological responses as disappointments and tragedies. The accelerated pulse and breathing are necessary for survival and also to pursue happiness. ▪ Worry, frustrations, and even petty irritations take a serious toll. During times of stress, your entire body moves into overdrive. With pounding heart and tightened muscles, you prepare to battle opponents, flee from danger, and take on the same kinds of extreme challenges encountered by your prehistoric ancestors. Your body's chemistry doesn't know the difference between the need to flee and the pressure to meet a deadline. It's no wonder so many people become ill when they're anxious or upset. ▪ Continual, long-term stress is damaging. A safe, nurturing home is more than a sanctuary; it is also a place for healing. Fresh air and plentiful sunlight are essential for our physical and emotional well-being. Sleep is as necessary as food to nourish our often neglected bodies. Water, in both the touch of a warm bath and the serene sound of a trickling fountain, is powerfully therapeutic. Genuinely relaxing design will assure that these needs are met so that everyone in the family will receive the rest and restoration necessary to take on life's challenges.

🌳 | **serenity secret #28**

Take a brisk walk. Even if you have only a few minutes to spare, a quick walk around the neighborhood will reduce the level of stress-producing hormones in your blood. Also, the aerobic activity will boost your energy, making you better able to withstand pressures at work and home.

---

opposite *A simple row of chairs on a quiet porch provides opportunities for the fresh air and sunlight we require. Here, the soothing atmosphere is enhanced by a color scheme of muted blue grays, reflecting the calm lake beyond.*

above *An all-wool oriental rug brings color and warmth to natural, hardwood floors. Catercornered between expansive windows, the writing table is perfectly positioned for healing sunlight and soothing views.*

Easy Breathing

Simply breathing can make you tense and anxious if the air inside your home contains harmful irritants. To assure fresh air:

- *Use water-based paints and varnishes.*

- *Avoid wrinkle-resistant, stain-resistant fabrics; they are often treated with harmful chemicals.*

- *Choose solid wood; avoid furnishings and cabinets made of composition wood.*

- *Replace wall-to-wall carpeting with area rugs.*

- *Clean with vinegar, lemon juice, baking soda, and other natural ingredients.*

- *Ban cigarettes and cigars.*

- *Install HEPA air filters.*

---

serenity secret #29

Open a window. Breathe deeply, inhaling the fresh air and absorbing natural light from the Sun. Even when the weather is very cold, you'll feel more relaxed in rooms that are well ventilated. For added freshness, hang bed linens in the sunshine and use all-natural cleaning solutions made of lemon juice.

Fresh Air

Designing for health may begin with things you cannot see. It is nearly impossible to feel relaxed in a room that is too hot or too cold, so simply changing the setting on the thermostat can make a significant difference. If weather permits, opening a window to admit fresh air can quickly boost the spirits of everyone in the room. Installing systems to filter the air and water will help remove harmful pollutants. However, the most important step in creating healthy, nourishing spaces is to choose fabrics, furnishings, paints, and other materials that are free from synthetic chemicals.

Many products sold today emit vapors that can lead to a variety of ailments ranging from headaches to severe depression. Furnishings made with pressed wood and many types of wall-to-wall carpeting are especially problematic because of the adhesives they contain. Paints, varnishes, and many cleaning products will also contribute to the problem of indoor air pollution. To minimize headaches, breathing difficulties, and other stress-inducing ailments, seek products free of chemical irritants. Choose water-based paints over alkyd; vinegar-based cleaning solutions over ammonia; and fresh, natural scents over aerosol air fresheners.

Frequently, the healthiest materials are also the most alluring. There is something deeply satisfying about the warm grain of natural oak, the softness of untreated cotton, and the uncomplicated beauty of earth-hewn stone. While it would be difficult, if not impossible, to completely banish synthetics, each healthy choice you make will contribute toward a more pleasing and more restful environment.

The warmth and luxury of wall-to-wall carpeting may be difficult to resist, especially in the bedroom where bare feet crave a bit of luxury. Beware, however, that the synthetic fibers in many carpets can cause respiratory problems and a variety of other discomforts. Also, any floor covering that cannot be lifted up makes an easy home for allergy-aggravating dust and dust mites. Whenever possible, opt for area rugs instead of wall-to-wall installations. Choose carpeting made from all-natural materials and make sure that the carpet padding does not emit unpleasant or potentially harmful fumes.

Healing Sleep

The importance of natural cycles cannot be underestimated. Restful, undisturbed sleep allows the body to restore itself and also helps the mind resolve problems and receive insights through healing dreams. In turn, the effects of sleep deprivation are devastating, leading to chronic illness and debilitating emotional and psychological problems.

You do not need an elaborate or fussy room to achieve a deeply relaxing slumber. In fact, you are likely to sleep more peacefully in surroundings that are not overly complicated. If at all possible, choose a private space that is distant from street traffic and the bustle of household noise. Make sure that bedding is firm enough to support your spine without creating uncomfortable pressure points. When beds are shared, consider using mattresses that can be adjusted to individual needs. If you suffer back or neck pain, add a cervical pillow that follows the natural curves of your body. You may find that you can sleep more restfully on an austere futon or *onda* bed with unbleached cotton linens and a single flat head cushion.

The energy of objects around you will invade your dreams, so decorate sleeping areas with an eye toward simplicity, choosing details that evoke joyful memories. Place a bowl of fragrant lotus blossoms by the window or hang a hand-woven tapestry above the bed. To encourage harmony in relationships, set two bud vases or a paired set of photographs on the bureau. Clear away papers and other reminders of work and responsibilities, but do place a notebook and a beautiful fine point pen within easy reach. If you wake in the night, quickly jot down your dreams before they fade. In the morning's light they may suggest the solutions you are seeking.

serenity secret #30

Move your bed. The ancient Chinese art of *feng shui* teaches that we sleep more peacefully if the foot of the bed does not point directly toward a mirror or a door. Choose a location away from support beams, shelves, and other structural elements that might interrupt the even flow of energy. To foster a sense of security, place the headboard against a wall; leave enough room on both sides so sleep partners don't feel cramped.

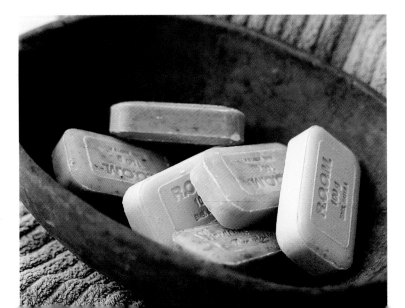

left *All-natural soaps and toiletries are gentle on the skin and kind to the spirit. Made from herbs, flowers, and other plants, they have no synthetic additives.*

"The thoughts of the day become the dreams of the night."

Chinese proverb

above *Books, papers, and other reminders of daytime responsibilities are easily tucked out of sight in this uncomplicated bedroom. A shallow alcove behind the bed displays dream-inspiring artwork.*

Touchable Textiles

It's easy to be enticed by modern wrinkleproof, stain-resistant fabrics. They seem to offer trouble-free luxury with a dazzling array of colors, patterns, and textures. Unfortunately, however, most miracle fibers contain synthetic substances that can make you feel sluggish or tense and irritable. For bedding, towels, curtains, upholstery, and rugs, the healthiest textiles are simple, natural spun fabrics.

Cotton

The slightly rumpled appearance of natural, untreated cotton has its own uninhibited beauty. Cotton is a soft, airy fiber that cools easily and dries quickly. Whisper-soft brushed cotton is a soothing choice for bedcoverings, while sturdy muslin and ticking fabric make attractive upholstery that will hold up under heavy family use. Sheer, light-filtering cotton gauze creates a romantic or exotic atmosphere when draped from windows or billowing over bedposts.

Linen

Made from the waxy flax plant, linen is sturdier than cotton and much more durable than factory-made synthetic fibers. This is the magic fabric of the Egyptians; linen found in ancient tombs is still intact. Dyed linen is bright and shimmering, while linen in its natural state takes on a lustrous, creamy hue that grows softer and more beautiful each time it is washed. Although very durable, linen wrinkles easily, so you may prefer to use it for curtains rather than cushions.

Silk

Lustrous and elegant, silk is spun from the sensuously smooth cocoon of the silk worm. Silk sounds like its name, creating a pleasing swish each time it is moved. Its shimmering surface makes silk especially lovely when cascading from windows or gathered into poofy valances. Unlike cotton, which dries rapidly, silk is highly absorbent and can be dyed to vivid colors. Bright sunlight may cause fading, however. Silk is an indulgence best confined to peaceful, dimly lit spaces.

Wool

Made from the coats of sheep, goats, camels, and other animals, wool is naturally insulating and often remarkably soft. Wool fibers are slightly curled, giving them a spongy quality that feels especially sumptuous under bare feet. Some of the world's most beautiful floor coverings—plush Persian rugs and brilliantly patterned carpeting from Turkey and the Far East—are woven from wool. Vacuum these rugs once a week to remove allergy-aggravating dust, and savor their cushioned comfort.

opposite *Health-conscious designers choose untreated cotton, linen, and other natural fibers for upholstery and curtains. Sisal and Chinese seagrass are healthy alternatives for carpeting.*

> **"Let the water settle; you will see the Moon and stars mirrored in your being."**
>
> Jalaluddin Rumi (1207–1273), Persian Sufi poet

Hydrotherapy

To turn your bathroom into a healing hot spring:

- *Surround the tub with plants, stones, and other reminders of nature.*

- *Eliminate outside noise; play recordings of soft music or sounds of rainfall.*

- *Fill your tub with steaming water.*

- *Add one cup of sea salt and one cup of bicarbonate of soda.*

- *Use a hand spray or running faucets to keep water circulating.*

- *Dim the lights.*

- *Soak for at least twenty minutes.*

- *Drink several glasses of fresh water.*

Healing Waters

The bathroom or home spa is without a doubt the most therapeutic region in the home. Even when space is extremely limited, bathing areas can become special places for relaxation and restoration. The rippling sounds of water echo our own natural rhythms and the warm moisture relieves muscle tension and calms the nerves. Ancient Greeks and Romans found comfort in hot springs bubbling up from the earth, and physicians in many cultures prescribed mineral baths to treat disease. Today, doctors often recommend hydrotherapy—water treatments—for a variety of ailments.

Compact saunas and whirlpools make it easy to transform nearly any bathroom into a luxurious spa. However, even a simple handspray attachment will turn a basic bathtub into a source of deeply soothing pleasure. And don't forget the guest bathroom: any bathing area that is seldom used can be refashioned for family use, giving each member of the household more time for uninterrupted soaking.

A truly healing bath begins with clean, pure water. Bacteria and other impurities can be absorbed through the skin when you bathe. Take wisdom from the age-old Japanese tradition of showering before you step into the tub. Also consider asking a professional testing laboratory for an analysis of the water from your tap. If lead, bacteria, or other contaminants are found, you may want to install water filters on your faucets or at the main inlet.

The most satisfying bathing areas are crafted from Earth-friendly materials. Quarried from mountains and canyons, marble, granite, and slate are more pleasing to the touch than artificial compounds such as fiberglass. Fired from earthen materials, ceramics, porcelain, and glass are reminiscent of river rocks and ocean-tossed stones. To create the sensation that you are bathing in warm, natural springs, cluster two or three smooth stones on the ledge of your bathtub. A blooming iris or pot of Boston fern will also help create the sense that you are swimming in a secluded grove. To enhance the atmosphere of cleanliness and abundance, add naturally scented soaps and an abundance of plush cotton bath towels.

left *Space is tight, but there's no shortage of luxury in this enticing bathing area. Sky blue walls and a cluster of plants and shells echo the scenic views outside.*

Peaceful Dining

We must eat to live, and we must eat well to live well. Healthy meals involve much more than good nutrition. How we eat can be nearly as important as what we eat. Every culture has its own rituals for the preparation and consumption of food. Books have been written, wars fought, and empires won and lost over the essential issue of cuisine and table manners.

The sharing of food is a potent symbol for peace and unity. Whether your dining area is a cozy alcove in the kitchen or a grand banquet hall with elaborate furnishings, it plays an important role. If you can organize family activities so that everyone comes together for a meal at least once a day, many conflicts will be eliminated or resolved. The dining area can be a place to talk, negotiate, and exchange ideas but not to quarrel. To this end, a certain amount of formality and routine is helpful. Maintain a consistent mealtime and a consistent seating arrangement. Children especially are comforted when they have their own chairs and, perhaps, special plates and cups they can call their own. To accentuate the sanctity of mealtime, you may want to put formal china and silverware into daily use. Place a heirloom tureen on the table, set linen napkins beside each plate, and light slim, elegant candles—one for each family member. Petty bickering, fussing, and trivial disputes tend to dissipate when there is an aura of awe and respect.

Few people today have time to prepare elaborate gourmet meals on a daily, or even a weekly, basis. However, a few extra moments to add small decorative touches will make a big difference in how a meal is received. Take inspiration from French Nouveau cuisine and serve modest portions artfully arranged with a colorful slice of fruit or a dash of sauce. Remember, also, Japanese traditions of serving meals in a series of small dishes beautifully arranged according to color and texture. Create peaceful palates with elegant, simple presentations.

Feng Shui Dining

The ancient Chinese art of feng shui teaches that the careful placement of tables and chairs will promote harmonious dining. Begin with these simple guidelines:

The Table
Avoid sharp corners. The most beneficial tables are round, oval, or octagonal. Wood is preferable to glass.

Chairs
Choose comfortable chairs with sturdy backs. An even number of seats at the table will seem less lonely, even if one chair remains unused. If possible, avoid seating diners with their backs toward windows or doors.

Seating Order
Each member of the family should sit in the appropriate place according to the ba-gua diagram.

- *Middle son: north*
- *Youngest son: northeast*
- *Eldest son: east*
- *Father: northwest*
- *Eldest daughter: southeast*
- *Middle daughter: south*
- *Mother: southwest*
- *Youngest daughter: west*

opposite *In an open floor plan, the kitchen flows smoothly into the dining area. Candles bring elegance and a sense of formality.*

serenity secret #31

Eat breakfast. Even if you are in a hurry, take time for a bowl of cereal or a piece of fruit. Leaping into day without food starves your cells, leading to headaches, low blood sugar, irritability, and anxiety. Moreover, skipping the morning meal will make you more susceptible to illnesses, adding even more stress to your life.

Ancient wisdoms often suggest that the dining area be placed away from the kitchen. The bustle of activity can be distracting, and heat and smoke will make it difficult to dine in peace. With careful planning, however, the kitchen can accommodate a serene area that celebrates the nurturing activities of preparing and serving food. Decorate the kitchen table with the same loving care you would use in a more formal dining room. Turn off the noisy dishwasher, place a crystal vase of fresh carnations on the table, and eat slowly, savoring the flavor and texture of every bite.

serenity secret #32

Imagine a flying moose. When anxious thoughts begin to overwhelm you, chase them away with a ridiculous image. Your mind can only hold one thought at a time, so each time you envision a moose with flapping wings, you are deflecting the thoughts that cause you stress. Remembering *moose wings* can also help when you are in the throes of a *mood swing*.

Assure Safety

- Use nightlights in halls and stairways; install motion-sensor lights outside.

- Place smoke detectors and carbon monoxide detectors near sleeping areas.

- Secure upstairs windows with protective rails.

- Install deadbolt locks on exterior doors.

- Ensure that all stairs have handrails.

- Provide a fire extinguisher in the kitchen.

- Place slip-resistant mats in the bathroom.

- Fasten grab bars near the bathtub and shower.

- Use ground-fault circuit interrupter (GFCI) outlets near sinks.

- Know how to shut off the electricity, gas, and water. Label the shut-off valves and switches.

- Assemble a first-aid kit with bandages, antiseptic, and other emergency supplies.

- Keep a flashlight and extra batteries in an easy-to-find location.

- Prepare a family evacuation plan; make sure all members know the fastest exits.

- Place emergency phone numbers in easy sight.

opposite *A simple wooden chaise and a few lovingly selected family photographs are all that's needed to create a tranquil "safe space" for private reflection.*

A Sense of Security

When you were a child, you may have created forts and tents out of tree branches, blankets, or packing crates. These cozy spaces fulfilled a basic human need for safety. Although you probably no longer wish to crawl into a closet or hide beneath the bed, you are likely to feel more relaxed when you know you are safe.

On the most fundamental level, security involves protecting members of the household from physical harm. Certainly every home should have adequate lighting in hallways and stairs, slip-resistant flooring in the bathroom, and smoke detectors in sleeping areas. Some families provide an additional layer of safety by creating specialized areas that will provide secure shelter in the event of a tornado, a hurricane, or acts of war.

An emergency shelter—a "safe room"—is ideally located in a basement with reinforced walls and ceilings or in a carefully constructed shelter that is securely anchored and strong enough to resist extreme winds. Creating this type of shelter is one way to relieve anxiety; simply knowing it is there can make news reports less frightening. Although it is designed for emergency use, there is no reason why a safe room cannot also serve as a library, family recreation room, or artist's retreat. Decorate the safe room as you would any other part of the home, filling it with colors and objects that bring you joy and hope.

The highest level of safety comes from the sense of caring and respect that only a loving, nurturing home can provide. Whether or not you choose to create an emergency shelter, you may want to establish a private "safe space" for each member of the family. A safe space is any part of the home specifically designed to provide comfort in times of high anxiety. An adult may find solace and escape in a quiet corner with a lamp and a chair, while a child might be drawn to a cozy nook beneath the stairs. If you are not sure where to place the safe spaces in your home, watch family patterns and observe where each person gravitates. A favorite color or a treasured memento will help personalize private areas. Hang a filmy strip of gauze or strings of glittering beads to establish magical boundaries. Let family members know that in this special place there can be no quarrels or complaining.

Chapter Eight

Earth, Sky, and Water

The world beyond our windows is so easy to forget. Ringing telephones and flickering computer monitors can make trees and birds, rivers, and fish seem distant and, perhaps, irrelevant to pressing daily needs. Yet, during times of trouble, there is nothing so comforting as a stroll through the park. Simply taking time to study a leaf or a shell will smooth away many of life's wrinkles. ▪ When you connect with nature, you are also connecting with your spiritual self. Homes designed for peaceful living often blur the boundaries between indoors and out with rooms that extend into gardens, flowers that bloom on window sills, and countless details that express an appreciation for earth, sky, and water. An intricately twisted scrap of driftwood on the mantel, a row of sea shells around the bathtub, or a cluster of sea-tossed stones on a side table help celebrate a world untouched by technology. ▪ One important way to embrace nature is through art. Beautifully grained woodcarvings, earthy clay sculptures, and evocative landscape paintings and prints can open the window to the imagination. Even if you are not an artist, you can contribute nature-inspired artworks to your décor. Gather photographs from your beach vacation into a series of sea-colored frames and assemble them in a grouping along with seashells and driftwood. Paint walls sea-inspired blues and greens to complement the aquatic theme. Or, choose a forest theme with framed prints of pressed leaves, leaf-stenciled fabrics, and an earthy palette of olive green and burnt umber. ▪ Also, don't forget the subtle influence of scents, sounds, and tactile sensations. Fresh flowers and aromatic herbs will stir thoughts of gardens and woodlands. For small, surprising whiffs of the outdoors, place small pots of growing mint or rosemary on your kitchen counter and nestle sachets of rose blossoms beneath the sofa cushions. Weather permitting, open your windows to fresh air and gentle breezes. Tingling wind chimes and a billowing curtain will announce the gentle movement of the air.

---

serenity secret #33

Find comfort in growing things. Fill hand-painted pots with heart leaf philodendron. The ancient Chinese art of *feng shui* teaches that plants with rounded green leaves will relieve financial worries. Modern scientists say that this lush, broad-leafed plant helps purify the air.

"The firm, the enduring, the simple, and the modest are near to virtue."

Confucius (551–479 B.C.), Chinese philosopher and spiritual leader

above *With leaf-print pillows and a flourishing philo-dendron plant, this sunny window seat seems to extend into the woods outside.*

Softening the Machines

Machines are an important part of nearly every modern home. Certainly we would be at a loss without refrigerators, washing machines, televisions, radios, and a host of other electrical conveniences. Yet, while they ease our labor and enhance our comfort, the things we plug in can also drain our spirits. With wires coursing behind walls, they send out electromagnetic currents that some researchers believe undermine our health and our ability to think clearly. Wireless devices such as cell phones can be especially disruptive, according to some reports. However, we don't need to ascribe to alarmist theories to know that we pay an emotional and spiritual price when we surround ourselves with mechanized metallics and cold, impersonal plastics.

Many superfluous devices such as electric can openers, juicers, and blenders can be eliminated without sacrificing a great deal of convenience. The machines we cannot do without will become less intrusive if they are

above *Neutral colors and details drawn from nature help soften the effects of modern technology in a bedroom and seating area. The television is mounted on adjustable wall brackets so it can be lowered for closer viewing.*

"**But what is happiness except the simple harmony between a man and the life he leads?**"

Albert Camus (1913–1960),
French author and philosopher

stored out of sight. Consider placing televisions and stereo equipment inside an antique oak armoire, or place them on shelves or brackets that can be raised toward the ceiling when they are not in use. Drape a cotton throw over the computer monitor and keep printers and copy machines behind a screen or in a closet. Sort out the tangle of electrical wires and tape them neatly to moldings behind the furniture.

Machines become less dominant in rooms decorated in ways that embrace nature. Paint walls muted colors inspired by the earth, sea, or sky. Combine high-tech equipment with wicker baskets, hand-woven tapestries, and timeworn oak chairs. Collect souvenirs from woodland walks or beach vacations and gather them into thematic groupings around the office machinery. Create minilandscapes inside a glass box or a glass-topped curio table. Or, design wall hangings and mobiles from branches, feathers, leaves, and dried flowers.

The scenes outside your windows will also help soften the machinery you keep indoors. Plan your lawn and garden with an eye to how the view will look from inside your house. Frame the composition with a beautiful garden sculpture or a trellis of climbing roses. Place low-voltage or solar lamps along garden paths to accent plantings after dark. If possible, park your car where it does not obscure natural views. If your windows face a neighbor's wall or a dreary parking lot, enhance the view with sheer lace curtains; stained glass; or large, wispy spider plants.

opposite *Wood, wicker, and clay mingle in this
profoundly peaceful space. Muted greens and
earthy golds suggest a quiet grove.*

"Adopt the pace of nature: Her secret
is patience."

Ralph Waldo Emerson (1803–1882),
U.S. philosopher, poet, essayist

Gifts from the Earth

Serene, Earth-embracing spaces are rich in details that suggest the patterns and textures of nature. Rugged, solid, and beautifully detailed materials from mountains, forests, and fields help us feel grounded in our own
lives. A floor made of fieldstone is certain to feel more satisfying than vinyl;
a chair carved from wood will satisfy in ways that plastic and chrome cannot. Consider all the surfaces inside your home—floors, walls, counters,
and furnishings—and explore the rich and varied alternatives offered by
Mother Nature.

From Mountains and Quarries

Stone is timeless. Slate and fieldstone evoke rugged mountainsides.
Soapstone suggests warmth and softness. Polished granite and creamy
marble and travertines remind us of grand palaces. With colors ranging
from black to yellow, green to red, natural stone can be tumbled or brush-
hammered for a rough texture, sandblasted for a matte gloss, or honed for
a soft satin sheen.

From Fire and Clay

We often associate tile with bathrooms, but the wide range of rich colors
and exquisite patterns make this durable material suitable for nearly any
room. Ceramic tile is made from clay and other earthen materials hardened
by intense heat. Because the color is fired deep into the clay, it is especially
resistant to scuffs and spills. Porcelain tile is rock-strong because it contains a large amount of quartz.

From Forests

For furnishings, floors, and paneling, nothing is as warm or as satisfying as
natural wood. Oak, cherry, ash, and maple each has its own special hue
ranging from honey gold to deep chocolate. Tropical woods such as teak
often have a smooth, fine grain that is both elegant and earthy.

From Fields and Marshes

For high-traffic areas, rugged floor mats made of grasses and reeds are
practical and durable. Harvested from coconut husk and woven into rustic
weaves, coir is inexpensive and strong enough to use for doormats.
Chinese seagrass and subtropical sisal are softer, with warm grassy hues
and lovely textures that resist stains and wear.

Earthen Mixtures

Although factory-made, cork and linoleum blend well in rooms designed to evoke nature. Cork is composed of tree bark and other Earth-friendly ingredients. Linoleum is a colorful mix of cork, clay, resins, and other materials. Both make pleasant choices for recreation areas because they are slightly resilient underfoot and they also help absorb sound. Moreover, cork and linoleum are biodegradable and generally free of toxins, making them preferable to vinyl.

The Wonder of Wood

From creamy white birch to coffee-black mahogany, wood is soothing and reassuring. Don't rule out nature's wonder material for kitchens and even bathrooms. Although water and moisture can damage wood, it will hold up surprisingly well under a few coats of strong, nontoxic finish. Also, wood that is scratched and marred can be surprisingly beautiful. Floors, paneling, and furnishings made of salvaged lumber are both lovely and forgiving: New scuffs simply add to their rich history.

Ash

With a straight grain and open pores, ash combines softness with strength, delicacy with shock resistance. Its low moisture content and properties of elasticity make this an easy wood to model into lightweight furniture or cabinets. Used as flooring, ash is pliable enough to resist continued punishment. Choose lustrous, almost-white ash for bright, contemporary design, or select a creamy brown for a rich, earthy decor and Old World charm.

Beech

Both European and American beech woods are hard, heavy, and strong, making them ideal for furniture and floors. The straight grain and fine, even texture of this silky smooth wood suggest stability and durability. With colors ranging from pale cream to almost-pink to ruddy brown, beech provides a beautiful accent for nearly any decor.

opposite *Architectural features create a strong sense of line and shape in a room designed for casual living. The timber framing mimics nature's rich patterns.*

Birch

Creamy white birch and darker red birch are silky smooth and tightly grained. Pin knots and small burls give these woods a sensuous fascination. For serene, neutral-toned rooms, combine white birch with sisal and crisp, unbleached linen.

Cherry

The ancient Greeks and Romans made furniture from this rich, red-brown wood, and today cherry is prized for its elegance and practicality. Cherry is very hard and quite lightweight; chairs and tables crafted from this silky

above *Unpainted wood is warm and forgiving; this sturdy table with its handy drawers brings comfort and practicality to an informal living area.*

"Every flower is a soul blossoming in Nature."

Gerard De Nerval (1813–1887), U.S. clergyman and abolitionist

wood can often be easily moved from room to room. Wine-toned upholstery and oriental carpets will enhance the ruddy color of your cherry furnishings. Time and sunlight will darken their hues.

Mahogany

Hewn in Africa and Honduras, polished mahogany is as dark and reflective as a midnight pond. Its fine grain seems to shift like ripples, shimmering as you change perspectives. For rooms that glimmer, mingle mahogany with brass or silver. For paneling and trim, consider using the less expensive Asian hardwood called Philippine mahogany. Technically this isn't a true mahogany, but its reddish brown surface can be finished to a satiny, mahoganylike sheen.

Maple

The name *maple* is derived from the Latin word for hard, and this remarkable wood truly will hold up under heavy use. Light creamy colored maple floors give any room a clean, open appearance. Blush colored maple is a warm and inviting complement to brick and terra-cotta.

Red Oak

With striking patterned grains that capture the sunlight, oak is very strong and fascinatingly beautiful. Floors and furnishings made from oak can have a warm, golden glow or a deep, earthy, brown sheen. Quartersawn oak is "rift cut" to reveal the intricate patterns of its growth rings. For a striking contrast, combine the rich texture of quartersawn oak with sleek, modern chrome or polished nickel.

Knotty Pine

Soft, lightweight pine has an informal, folksy quality. Ranging from nearly white to deep rust, this charming wood displays its beauty in eccentric spatters of pin knots and larger swirling bull's-eye patterns. Use pine floors and furnishings to evoke a comfortable, country atmosphere.

Walnut

The burls and curls on this treasured wood give endless fascination. Ranging from dusky beige to a nearly purple shade of brown, walnut grows more lustrous and increasingly beautiful as it ages. Celebrate nature's patterns by combining walnut with rustic clay pottery or tall vases of twigs and dried flowers.

Green Spaces

There is no worry so great that cannot be eased by watching green things grow. A garden, no matter how small, can become an important area for releasing stress and finding hope. Plant morning glory seeds in the patch of ground outside your kitchen door, fill window boxes with brilliant red geraniums, or set pots of gerbera daisies on the balcony. To add to the joy of creation, mingle ornamental plants with miniature tomatoes and other easy-to-grow vegetables.

While they feed the spirit, plants also benefit your physical health. Some researchers believe that certain varieties of ordinary foliage help cleanse the air. By placing several pots of English ivy, Chinese evergreen, or bamboo palm in every room, you set up your own miniature ecosystem for removing formaldehyde, carbon monoxide, and other harmful fumes. Find the sunniest windows inside your home and fill them with the pots of cheerful chrysanthemums or gentle, life-affirming peace lilies.

Fresh cut flowers will also bring a spirit of renewal provided that the water is changed often. *Feng shui* wisdom and common sense suggest that wilting plants will sap energy from the room, so make sure to replace fading flowers with fresh blooms. Bring in branches of forsythia and watch them blossom, float fragrant lotus blossoms in a crystal bowl, and tuck bud vases with baby's breath in sleepy corners of your home. Choose flowers for their colors and also for their fragrances. A whiff of lilac or gardenia will quickly lighten the spirits of all who enter.

To create a small heaven on your Earth, look for spaces that can be transformed into an indoor garden. The obvious location is an enclosed sunporch; however, you can create a green room anywhere there is light and ventilation. Consider a window alcove, a utility room, or even a garage. If sunlight is limited, illuminate the area with artificial "grow lights" that radiate the ultraviolet rays plants need. Spend time each day in your small jungle of potted vines and hanging bougainvillea. Water them lovingly and tell them your worries. By nourishing your plants you will also nourish your soul.

Fragrant Flowers

To fill your home with joyful aroma, bring in blooms from these plants:

- *Chrysanthemum*
- *Gardenia*
- *Honeysuckle*
- *Jasmine*
- *Lilacs*
- *Lily of the valley*
- *Magnolia*
- *Marigolds*
- *Orange blossoms*
- *Orchids*
- *Peonies*

opposite *A trellis of climbing roses can transform a small brick patio into a miniature paradise. Abundant flowers, a cushioned chaise lounge, and a basket of favorite magazines make this green space especially inviting.*

🌳 | **serenity secret #37**

Adopt a pet. Researchers say that the simple, repetitive motion of petting a dog or cat will lower your blood pressure and boost your levels of serotonin, an important hormone that helps ward off depression.

Creature Comforts

We share our planet with four-legged creatures and creatures that fly, swim, or crawl. Inviting favorite animals into your life is an important way to stay in tune with nature's rhythms. If you have a yard or garden, plant flow-ers that will lure butterflies. Place birdbaths and bird feeders within easy view from your home. Be sure to hang ribbons or bits of foil outside your windows so feathered friends won't fly into the glass.

Inside your home, birds can be a continual source of joy and inspiration. Because of their easy flight and seeming weightlessness, canaries and finches seem to represent the eternal spirit. Talking birds such as parrots and some parakeets are endlessly entertaining, while a variety of exotic tropical birds serve as brilliant reminders of life's complexity. Let these beautiful birds fill your home with color and song or chatter. A tall, orna-mental wire cage that mimics a gilded palace can become a dazzling focal point. If the area is secure, occasionally open the cage and let your birds flutter around the room.

Fish bring their own quiet pleasures. We are quickly soothed watching the hypnotic, fluid movement of iridescent tropical fish. An aquarium will become a soothing center of interest in a quiet, dimly lit room. To enhance the peaceful aquatic atmosphere, paint your walls watery shades of blue and turquoise. In ancient Eastern thought, golden carp represented wealth. Create a small pond—indoors or out—and take time to watch the soothing motion of these swirling fish.

Rabbits, guinea pigs, hamsters, ferrets, cats, and dogs are mammals like ourselves. When we share our homes with these warm-blooded crea-tures, we awaken our instincts to nurture and protect. Ironically, by giving care we also receive care. Instinctively, we are comforted by the rhythmic motion and tactile pleasure of grooming animal companions, and the daily interaction with a trusting, completely accepting being reinforces our own self-confidence.

In some traditions, animals represent our guides on the spiritual plane. When we share our lives with a dog or cat, or even a snake or iguana, we acknowledge our own primal natures and discover important aspects of our souls. If you are not in touch with animal nature inside yourself, you may feel a vague sense of loss or an emptiness you can't quite explain. Try introducing the spirit of a favorite animal by displaying a symbolic carving or painting. Viewing a sculpture of a horse or a dolphin will awaken feelings and attributes associated with that animal. Even a child's stuffed toy can help arouse feelings of power or tenderness.

Earth Friendly

Our homes are our sanctuaries, but we do not live in isolation. Whether we are painting a wall or upholstering a chair, we are making decisions that will ultimately impact the environment. Natural, nonsynthetic fabrics such as untreated cotton are Earth-friendly because they do not add toxic chemicals to the air and water. Biodegradable materials like wood and clay also express respect for nature because they decompose when their useful lives have ended.

Just as the ancients taught, all things in the universe are connected. When we are kind to the world, we are also being kind to ourselves. A sense of peace comes from switching off the unused light, repairing the dripping faucet, and turning down the heat in an empty room. We are likely to feel more in harmony with the world at large when we conserve water and electricity and choose appliances for their energy efficiency. Simple tasks such as recycling bottles are life affirming because they help preserve and protect the environment we need for our own survival.

This spirit of conservation does not mean turning away from creature comforts or living a life of grueling self-denial. The goal is not to add additional sources of stress but to design nourishing spaces that provide a deeper level of fulfillment. When we adopt practices of Earth-friendly design, we begin to create meaningful spaces that will provide years, and perhaps centuries, of comfort and productive use. Instead of grasping at every passing fashion trend, we take joy in preserving the things we already have.

Ultimately, the most beautiful and the most spiritually satisfying possessions are the ones that will bear the test of time. A solidly built chair, handed down through generations, is kinder to the world and more pleasing to the spirit than a short-lived plastic piece that will soon be sent to a landfill. Meals served on aged china—even if there are a few chips—are more satisfying and more meaningful than food dished up on throwaway plates. By recycling and repurposing our possessions, we reduce the drain on natural resources and feel more at peace with ourselves and with the world.

above *In an austere setting, plants grouped in a tight cluster create a sense of abundance. The brilliant green pillows suggest the vitality and excitement of new growth.*

left *Sunlight shimmers through pergola-style skylights, warming earth-quarried floors in a bathing area that celebrates nature. Water-saving faucets and insulated windows help conserve resources.*

🌳 | **serenity secret #38**

Knock on wood. Touch a tree. Feel the texture and temperature of solid, earthen things. When life feels uncertain, let the sensations in your fingers remind you that the world has substance, form, and meaning. Say a prayer of thanks.

Chapter Nine

Storage and Display

"It is preoccupation with possessions, more than anything else, that prevents us from living freely and nobly."
Bertrand Russell (1872–1970), English philosopher, mathematician, and writer

A whirlwind of confusion and disarray is almost unavoidable in an active household where parents and children simultaneously pursue work, play, and hobbies. The business of daily living creates tidal waves of papers. Tables and countertops quickly become cluttered with magazines, craft supplies, schoolbooks, stray buttons and coins, and various other items dropped in haste. Cherished collections and sentimental souvenirs also add to the chaos as they gather dust, call out for polishing, or simply get in the way. ▪ There is no question that disorder provokes stress, and there is no shortage of advice on how to best organize a household. Countless books and articles grapple with the problem of clutter and, for compulsive collectors, there are seminars on clutter containment and a variety of self-help therapy groups. Capitalizing on the trend, one company even sells Clutter Clearer bells: Hang the satin cord over the mess and will yourself to remove it. Devices like this are not totally absurd because controlling clutter really is a matter of focusing attention and making a decision. ▪ Often the decision can be surprisingly difficult. Things that are seemingly useless can feel essential emotionally, bringing comfort and reassurance. Keys left on the counter tell us that someone is home, a ticket stub reminds us of a happy evening at the theater, and a tumbling pile of magazines implies that the information we need is close at hand (if only we could find it). ▪ The process of organizing a household calls for a close look at family habits and also a bit of self-analysis. You will see less clutter and encounter fewer family conflicts if mess-producing activities are given their own special places. Choose a single area for paying bills and doing routine paperwork. Select another area for working on crafts, and still another area for watching television. These work and play areas need not be spacious. Simply putting boundaries around family activities will minimize confusion and help maintain a sense of order. A folding screen, a curtain made from beads or shells, concentrated task lighting, or a brightly colored area rug may be all you need to signal the transition between spaces.

above *A narrow shelf along the dining room wall provides display space for this calming collection of art and pottery. Neutral colors and matching frames let the artwork become the center of attention.*

Be sure to take time to think about the reasons why papers end up on the dining room table, why shoes pile up in the hall, and why no one is ever able to find the scissors. A regular, dependable system for sorting through belongings will do more to bring order than the most impressive storage cabinet. Deciding what to store, what to display, and what to discard can become a meaningful family activity, encouraging open conversation, resolving conflicts, and clarifying values and priorities.

Comings and Goings

The entrance to your home is the passageway between worldly worries and family comforts. A serene entry foyer with soothing neutral colors and restful diffused lighting will ease the transition. A painting or small sculpture will express family tastes and interests, reminding everyone who enters about the things most important in the household.

The entry foyer also plays a key role in household clutter control. A roomy closet is always desirable, but even a row of wicker baskets and a few sturdy wall pegs will help confine coats, hats, keys, and handbags. Be sure to place a doormat at the entrance and to provide a chair or bench so that family and visitors can sit down to remove their shoes. Make sure that passageways are free of obstructions and that doors swing open easily, without sticking or banging into furniture. Keep in mind that adjacent doors will create jarring collisions if they open into each other. To economize on space, replace interior doors with pocket doors or curtains.

For many families, the main traffic to and from the home is not through the formal entry way but through a garage, utility room, or mud room, usually at the back of the house. Family members who must continually squeeze past baskets of laundry or garbage pails are likely to feel a higher level of tension. A quick way to lift the spirits of everyone in the household is to treat the rear entryway with a fresh coat of paint and to make sure the space is well illuminated. A flourishing philodendron in a beautiful ceramic pot or a gently sounding wind chime can also do much to improve the temperament of everyone who passes through this space. Unsightly laundry machines, paint cans, and lawn equipment should be hidden behind a curtain or a folding screen.

Control Clutter

- *Observe where messes accumulate and create storage in that area.*

- *Provide chests, cabinets, or hooks by entry doors.*

- *Set aside areas for mess-producing activities.*

- *Create a lost-and-found box to stow misplaced items.*

- *Each time you acquire something new, discard something you don't want or need.*

- *Establish a routine for clutter clearing; mark appointed times on the family calendar.*

- *Involve the entire family in clean-up efforts.*

🌳 | **serenity secret #39**

Open a drawer. Find one thing you have not used this year. Throw it away. Creating clean, uncluttered spaces does not have to be an overwhelming chore. Instead, make shedding the unnecessary a daily habit, as quick and easy as opening a window blind.

opposite *Soft green colors and bright, diffused lighting establish a calming atmosphere in this informal, rear entryway. Hooks along the wall hold coats and hats; a storage bin beneath the window keeps garden tools out of the way.*

At the Entryway:

- *Place a sturdy coir or jute mat by the door.*
- *Install light switches within easy reach.*
- *Provide a handsome wooden bench for seating and storage.*
- *Create storage nooks beneath stairways.*
- *Stow children's belongings in low cubbyholes.*
- *Combine utilitarian coat hooks with a colorful display of hats.*
- *Include a decorative chest or cabinet with a shallow drawer for mail and catalogs.*
- *Set an elegant handcrafted basket on a low table to catch keys.*
- *Choose artwork and decorative details that reflect family values.*
- *Assure that display shelving is secure; avoid placing fragile items near high traffic areas.*
- *Post messages of welcome and encouragement.*

A helpful tool for clutter control is to think of the area around the family entrance as the "customs headquarters" for the household. Every item that enters the home must first pass through this space, so the point of entry is the logical place to ask pressing questions about whether new possessions are truly needed or desired. Place a sign or a symbolic detail at the family entrance to remind each household member that rejecting nonessentials will be easier if done before they are brought inside.

The family entrance is a useful location for a family message board and calendar. Use this space to post practical reminders related to household duties, to coordinate family activities, and also to share messages of love and inspiration. A friendly note that says, "Easy does it" or simply, "Relax!" can help calm stressed family members as they race in and out the door.

above *A basket by the door catches clutter before it makes its way into the house. Shelves are handy for stowing shoes, caps, and keys.*

"One can furnish a room very luxuriously by taking out furniture rather than putting it in."

Francis Jourdain (1876–1958), French decorator

Starting Your Day

A large family with only one or two bathrooms is likely to encounter conflicts as individuals wait their turns. A tangle of brushes and cosmetics on the counter or a pile of damp towels on the floor can also be a source of irritation. A bathroom that is disorganized will turn simple grooming into a stressful event, stirring up enough tension to spoil an entire day.

To minimize frustrations and disputes, create spaces outside the bathing area for shaving, hairstyling, and other routine grooming tasks. Make sure that each family member has a private dressing area, a brightly lit mirror, and drawers for brushes, combs, and cosmetics. If possible, choose a small room or walk-in closet with a door that closes. Line the walls with eastern red cedar to repel moths and other pests, or toss a few chips of this aromatic wood into linen drawers. To wake up the fragrance in cedar paneling, give it a light sanding every few years.

To save steps, you may want to design spaces that combine dressing and grooming with routine household tasks. A sewing room or a laundry center are ideal settings for a vanity table and a wardrobe for clothes storage. However, you do not need a large home to create private dressing areas. A corner of the bedroom, concealed behind a folding screen, can become an appealing space.

A well-planned grooming area will provide storage for many items traditionally kept in the bathroom. Extra towels and laundry hampers are better off away from steamy bathroom environments; move these to dressing rooms or bedrooms. Medications also should be stored in a secure, dry place. Clean out the bathroom medicine cabinet, discard any medications that have expired, and place any remaining prescription medicines in a childproof vanity drawer belonging to the person who will be using them. A first-aid kit with medicines used by everyone in the household is best located in the kitchen or pantry. Whether you are storing medicines or throwing them away, always make sure small children cannot reach them.

As you plan dressing rooms and grooming centers, think beyond functionality. Even when space is limited, the place where you keep clothing and intimate items can become a very special, private retreat. Use the dressing area to display inspirational pieces that will launch the day with a cheerful attitude. Set a vase of baby's breath on the vanity table, display antique family photos in filigreed frames, and arrange a collection of crystal perfume bottles on glass shelves. Perhaps the grooming center can also become your "safe space" where you retreat for quiet reflection during times of high anxiety. Bring in your favorite chair and a treasured book, and provide a small cassette or CD player to fill this space with soothing music.

Planning Your Grooming Center

- *Consider combining the dressing area with a sewing room or laundry center.*

- *Supply a comfortable chair and a well-illuminated mirror.*

- *Set laundry hampers nearby.*

- *Provide a combination of rods and shelves.*

- *Use wall pegs for robes and workclothes.*

- *Store out-of-season clothing in a separate area.*

- *Find additional storage spaces in the hallways between bed and bath.*

- *Add artwork and decorative details that comfort and inspire.*

🌳 | **serenity secret #41**

Put on your party clothes. Spend an ordinary day at home wearing your most flattering outfit and favorite cologne. Simply putting on a special piece of jewelry will boost your spirits and heighten your sense of self-worth.

opposite *Your closet need not be for storage alone. Display shelving and a comfortable chair transform a utilitarian bedroom closet into an appealing dressing room.*

Work and Play

Despite all the best efforts, messes happen. Catalogs pile up on tabletops, craft activities scatter flecks of paper on the floor, and children's toys wind up on the stairs. The best way to maintain order in a busy household is to make sure that the messiest activities are given their own dedicated areas with plenty of storage space for supplies. To tame the chaos in offices, art studios, sewing areas, carpentry shops, and anywhere family members pursue messy hobbies, look for desks and cabinets with doors and drawers. A rolltop desk or an armoire will let you tuck away equipment and unfinished work. Apothecary drawers are handy for storing pens, brushes, scissors, and small tools.

Chances are, you will find that your work is more productive and your creativity flows more freely when your desk or table is cleared of items not essential to the task at hand. However, don't overlook the power of inspirational artwork and mementos. Place within easy view a photograph of someone you admire, a meaningful slogan, a trophy, or other symbol of accomplishment.

In a household with young children, toys and games will easily make their way to every corner. Confining play to a specified room can help maintain order, yet it's not usually desirable to isolate children from the rest of the family. A better solution is to establish several designated play areas so that the children can be easily supervised. Instead of storing toys in the child's bedroom, set roomy toy bins in key areas such as the kitchen, laundry room, and family room. Keep crayons and paints in a drawer close to where children usually sit to draw or paint.

Children grow rapidly and quickly change interests, so set aside time twice a year to pack away or donate unwanted toys. Do be sure, however, to save a few treasured items. Many years later, a stuffed bear or a model car will be a happy reminder of the child's youth and innocence.

---

serenity secret #42

Start a keepsake closet. Gather together snapshots, letters, diplomas, drawings, small toys, greeting cards, birth announcements, and other mementos. Don't worry if you can't find time to organize your treasures chronologically. Label what you can and place the items together on a shelf or inside a sturdy archival box. Add a sachet of herbs or a bar of soap with a fragrance that evokes warm memories. Visit your keepsake closet whenever life seems uncertain; your souvenirs from the past will provide a comforting sense of continuity.

"Our life is frittered away by detail. Simplify, simplify."

Henry David Thoreau (1817–1862),
U.S. author and philosopher

right *With shimmering wood paneling and minimal decoration, this austere space provides freedom for creative pursuits. The functional bench folds out into a bed. Cabinets at each end help keep papers and supplies orderly.*

"Hominess is not neatness."

Witold Rybczynski, contemporary, Scottish-born
Canadian architect, educator, and author

above and right *Centered in an expansive, open living area, a sturdy, handcrafted sofa evokes a sense of stability. Displayed on the side table and in the cabinet, decorative details drawn from several cultures bring a sense of history and heritage. Large collections remain orderly when they are rotated, displaying only a few items at a time.*

Affirm Your Heritage

- *Combine the essence of different cultures. Identify a mixed family heritage by bringing together representative colors and patterns—the blue and white simplicity found in a Greek village with the yellow and blue patterns of southern France.*

- *In colors and textures, combine the natural elements of different homelands— bamboo and redwood, thistle and rubber, granite and clay, shamrock and lotus.*

- *Create collections that express the singular or mixed heritage that is your family—shells, stones, dried flowers, fruit.*

- *Mix the architectural and interior designs from different time periods: Display ancient masks in a modern loft, Japanese furnishings in a remodeled country barn.*

- *Be whimsical; dare to include eccentric details and unexpected combinations.*

Living Spaces

We do not assemble our lives in matched suites of ready-made coordinates. The things that we cherish come to us in bits and pieces: a favorite chair from a grandparent, a settee from an out-of the-way antique shop, a vase from a beloved friend. And then there is the chaos of colors and patterns—the cushions and upholstery and pillows and carpets and wallpaper. A room that is truly lived in is certain to feel the impact of everyone who spends time there. With details that reflect differing tastes, interests, and personalities, the atmosphere may be warm and comforting, or merely chaotic. How do we achieve peace when our lives are rich, full, and— possibly—confused?

Warm, welcoming living areas strike a balance between order and disorder. Sometimes you may need to strip away extraneous details, and sometimes you will want to forgive them. The challenge of harmonizing elements that are very different can be a meaningful way to affirm the value of each person, promoting family harmony. Feel free to mix accessories that express individual personalities and interests. Combine an antique fishing buoy with handpainted ceramics. Incorporate artwork that suggests a sense of cultural heritage. Diverse collections will seem more orderly if you arrange them according to color, size, or material. For a grouping of prints or paintings, choose matching picture frames.

Simplifying the space around collections can also help the room seem less cluttered. Remove heavy carpets and curtains. Paint walls a neutral color and let displays of photographs and artwork become the focus of attention. If the room begins to feel overcrowded and claustrophobic, consider taking the approach used by museums: Choose just a few items and change the displays periodically. Groupings in multiples of three— three sculptures, six paintings, etc.—will bring a sense of balance and order. The activity of selecting and setting up new "exhibits" can become a lively family activity, similar to decorating the house for a holiday.

Cooking and Dining

There is something alluring about a kitchen. Regardless of its size or décor, family and guests are often drawn to its warm aromas, bustling activity, and cheerful informality. Surrounded by pots, bowls, utensils, and heavy appliances, neighbors trade gossip, spouses talk about their day, children call for attention, and busy cooks try to go about their job of preparing meals. This confusing mix of activities can be delightful, but if the space is not well planned, there are certain to be moments of discord and noisy confrontation.

Kitchens are repositories for a large quantity of paraphernalia. One of the most important decisions you'll need to make is whether to display cooking equipment or to conceal it. Cabinets with wooden or frosted glass doors will give the space a clean, uncluttered appearance and also minimize the need for dusting. On the other hand, pots and utensils are easier to reach when they hang from hooks or sit on open shelves. Cooking equipment that is openly displayed also does double duty, becoming decorative as well as functional.

If space allows, you may find it helpful to think of the kitchen as a second living room. Place a pot of hibiscus beneath a growlight on the counter and soften utilitarian linoleum or vinyl floors with a bright area rug. Create a cozy reading corner with an upholstered chair and footstool. Line one wall with open shelving and mingle novels with the cookbooks. A larger kitchen can also become a lively family entertainment center with the television and stereo equipment tucked inside an antique hutch. Since water is readily available, the kitchen can even become a convenient studio for painting or mess-producing crafts.

right *A small kitchen at the center of family activity can become a second living room. Books, family photographs, and potted plants make this space cozy and inviting. The work island saves steps and minimizes the stress of preparing and serving meals.*

opposite *Preparing meals and socializing combine when the kitchen is open to the living area. Illuminated by pendant lamps, the long counters supply ample work and dining space with storage below.*

Lighten the Workload in Every Room:

- *Choose simple furnishings without detailed spindles or carvings.*

- *Replace wall-to-wall carpeting with easy-to-wash area rugs.*

- *Remove shoes before entering the house.*

- *Replace pleated curtains and venetian blinds with easy-clean window shades.*

- *Display china, crystal, and other dust-collectors in glass cases.*

- *Hang photographs on walls instead of displaying them on tables and shelves.*

- *Set aside special areas for mess-producing activities.*

- *Store items near where they will be used.*

- *Put baskets or boxes in each room to catch clutter.*

- *Use just a few multipurpose cleaning products.*

- *Schedule specific days for housecleaning; delegate tasks to each family member.*

- *Play music while you clean: your spirits will lift and the work will go faster.*

A narrow galley kitchen will be too small to accommodate this much activity; however, you may be able to carve out space in a nearby dining room. A window or passthrough between the kitchen and the adjacent room will allow conversation to flow freely between the two spaces. Upholstered chairs set slightly away from the dining table will encourage family and visitors to linger there.

All too often, formal dining rooms take on the forlorn appearance of a space that is too seldom used. To pull some of the warmth and energy of the kitchen out into the dining area, choose colors and decorative details that integrate the two areas. Consider displaying seldom-used copper cookware on the sideboard and use a wheeled cart to transport china and silverware back and forth. Uncomplicated, functional items associated with food bring a very special kind of comfort. Displayed on open shelves or inside glass cabinets, plates and platters combine simple beauty with the reassuring reminder that we are in a safe place where we will be nurtured and loved.

Chapter Ten

Deeper Meanings

"We do not see things as they are, we see them as we are."
The Talmud

Every object in the home has a story. It tells the tale of its creation, the memories of how it was acquired, and the hopes and dreams it inspires. The wing-backed chair passed down through the family still holds the aroma of grandfather's pipe. And while the chair evokes the sense of his presence, it also reminds us of his loss, the parceling out of his belongings, and possibly hurtful family arguments. As much as the chair is weighted with a past, it also holds a future; perhaps it represents a desire to emulate his wisdom and kindness, or a wish to recreate a family closeness that has been lost. ▪ Whenever you make changes in your home, you are not merely rearranging the furniture; you are also rewriting your personal history. Moving a bookcase or throwing away a tattered rug can set off a string of events, affecting everyone in the household. Clearing away a stack of unread magazines evokes a sense of freedom that inspires the struggling artist to start a new project. Repainting a wall brings a brightness that prompts a grieving widow to move on with her life. And, inexplicably, setting a vase of freshly cut lilacs on the bureau soothes a fussy infant. ▪ Layered on top of the personal associations, possessions also suggest archetypal meanings that barely register on the subconscious. A circular cushion may represent life's eternal cycle, a stone bowl may symbolize stability, and a solid oak table may suggest creation, growth, and nourishment. When you dream, the various parts of your home can take on important symbolic roles, the attic representing hidden memories and the kitchen representing creativity and nurturing. According to the psychotherapist Carl Jung, your dwelling is a physical manifestation of your psyche; changes to the home reflect changes to the self. ▪ Redecorating is an important way to manage stress because with every small transformation, you are actually working on your own interior design.

opposite *In this eclectic living area, objects are selected for their symbolic significance. A zebra print ottoman, a bronze sculpture, and a historic portrait convey special meanings for a family of collectors.*

"Simplicity is the ultimate sophistication."

Leonardo da Vinci (1452–1519), Italian Renaissance
artist and scientist

opposite *A balanced arrangement of matching chairs
creates a sense of calm and order. Fitting perfectly
in the angular alcove, the square table holds a single,
simple centerpiece.*

In Times of Excess Responsibility . . .

Ringing telephones. Crying babies. Bills to pay, papers to write, meals to prepare, and meetings to attend. Often it seems that there is no relief from the
frantic pace of an ordinary day. The things that have deep, lasting value—
family, creative pursuits, spirituality—are pushed aside in the hubbub of frantic
activity. Meals are skipped, sleep is lost, and, without proper nutrition and rest,
it becomes increasingly difficult to meet deadlines and make clear decisions.

When life becomes too busy and too complicated, it is time to simplify
your home décor. Clear away the clutter that rattles at your nerves; embrace
minimalist design. Choose uncomplicated patterns and neutral colors: cream,
pearl gray, and dusty pastels. Use simple shapes and straight lines to create
a sense of order and direction. Remove bulky fabric window treatments and
set fruit in an orderly arrangement on the kitchen counter. Seek symmetry.
Place a single small table between matching chairs. Remove furnishings that
are rarely used and collections that merely gather dust. You will begin to feel
a sense of freedom simply by creating clean, open spaces.

■ **Where to Begin**

Seek Simplicity

When you are feeling exhausted and overwhelmed by responsibilities and
obligations:

- Clear obstacles from passageways.
- Minimize collections and decorative details.
- Combine light, neutral colors with the golden tones of natural wood.
- Remove light-obscuring window treatments; fill rooms with
  soul-warming sunlight.
- Replace wall-to-wall carpeting with natural pine, oak, maple, or ash.
- Choose lightweight, functional tables, shelves, and seating.
- Emphasize confident, straight lines.
- Seek symmetrical, balanced arrangements.
- Add the calming fragrance of cedar or marjoram.
- Ensure that all doors and windows open easily, even if you
  never use them.

In Times of Insecurity
and Worry . . .

May you live in interesting times is the ancient saying that has become the double-edged sword of the modern world. Information technology has created a global village, expanding our awareness and also our fears. Satellites spin around the Earth, transmitting waves of digital information about desert armies. World events seem beyond our control, yet they impact our lives. Stability that we once knew, or thought we knew, seems elusive. We may discover that we can no longer count on the security of a job, the refuge of a relationship, the solidity of our health, the permanence of our money supply, or the seemingly good intentions of the person next-door.

When the stress of interesting times disrupts the harmony of your home, seek comfort in art, treasured heirlooms, and objects that bring you joy. Instead of an austere, minimalist environment, you may need paintings on the wall, a cluster of smooth onyx carvings, and favorite books stacked beside a molded chair. Incorporate circular forms and soft, rounded shapes. Let in sunlight, but provide translucent blinds to filter out the afternoon glare. Soften floors with textured woolen rugs. Find comfort in the repeated colors and patterns of floral prints or decorative stenciling. Most importantly, indulge yourself with a crystal vase of fragrant roses or gardenias and listen closely to nature's healing music.

■ Where to Begin
Find Comfort

During times of worry and insecurity:

- Seek soothing *yin* energy: choose flowing lines and soft, graceful forms.
- Fill elegant crystal vases with blooming roses and other fragrant flowers.
- Create cozy, comforting nooks with soft cushions and reassuring sunlight.
- Combine warm amber hues with deeply soothing shades of pink and rose.
- Provide soft, diffused lighting.
- Cover floors with colorful woven rugs.
- Develop a motif of repeated patterns and colors.
- Display family photographs, paintings, and treasured artifacts.
- Store newspapers and newsmagazines out of sight.
- Remove televisions from bedrooms, kitchens, and dining areas.

🌳 | serenity secret #45

Laugh. Exchange jokes with friends or watch a comedy on television. The humor will lift your spirits and the laughter will actually change your body chemistry. Your level of stress hormones—cortisol and adrenaline— will decrease, and you'll feel less bothered by irritations and better able to handle frustrations.

"A man's fortune must first be changed from within."

Chinese proverb

opposite *The city beyond this high-rise window is a constant reminder of worldly pressures and anxieties. Inside, however, rounded shapes and soft, golden hues create a soothing atmosphere. The pink rose blossoms are echoed on the painted chair.*

"Enjoy to the full the resources that are within thy reach."

Pindar (c. 518–438 B.C.), Greek lyrical poet

left *Fresh flowers, an elegant vase, and a row of crystal bottles bring luxury to this pleasant bathing area. An expansive wall mirror captures the sunlight and reflects peaceful views.*

opposite *Gold, copper, and bronze suggest luxury, yet they are earthy and sensual. To create an aura of comfort and ease, define your space with a folding screen painted in luminescent metallics.*

In Times of Frustration . . .

All too often, what disrupts our inner peace is not the weighty world events but life's petty annoyances. The ringing of a cell phone or booming music from the house next door intrude into our private space. A missing paycheck, a tardy employee, a traffic jam, and countless other delays and inconveniences try our patience. A broken light switch, a baffling computer program, or an uncooperative teenager can push us to the edge.

To ease the stress of life's petty annoyances and frustrations, concentrate on redirecting the flow of energy—*chi*—through your home. Sense the emotional tenor of each room and of each occupant. Insulate your home against noise and distractions, repair or dispose of broken appliances, and develop a system for keeping pesky piles of papers from collecting on the kitchen table. Then, to ease your nerves and calm your spirit, seek ways to indulge yourself and your family. Suggest abundance with warm, metallic colors: copper, bronze, brass, and gold. Focus on sensual details. Introduce textures that entice the sense of touch and fill rooms with the soothing fragrances of sage and sandlewood. Turn your bathroom into a center for hydrotherapy and your bedroom a haven for love.

■ **Where to Begin**
Nourish the Senses

When petty annoyances rattle at your serenity:

- Combine lush metallic colors with uncomplicated lines and shapes.
- Seek the cool sensuality of smooth marble, glass, steel, and brass.
- Use oversized mirrors to capture pleasing views.
- Place seating areas where they will receive the most sunlight.
- Emphasize luxury in bathing areas; provide plenty of plush towels and scented soaps.
- Design for sensuality in the bedroom; set fragrant candles on the bureau and hang a light-capturing crystal in the window.
- Repair leaky faucets, squeaky doors, and other sources of irritation.
- Replace flickering fluorescent lights with soothing incandescent fixtures.
- Turn off computers and other electronic equipment when not in use.
- Mask outside noise with recordings of falling rain, or make your own music through singing, chanting, or drumming.

In Times of Conflict . . .

Wherever two or more people live together under a single roof, conflicts will occur. Lifemates may disagree over anything from finances to fidelity, while children learning to express their independence will inevitably quarrel with their parents. Within the extended family called a nation, religion and politics are continual sources of discord. Moreover, internal conflicts—indecision and mixed emotions—are a common source of stress for every thinking person.

When you find your stress mounting because of family disagreements, it is time to seek harmony in home design. Look for ways to unify rooms with color, pattern, and texture. Spiraling lines and curving forms will help draw together different elements in a room. Choose artwork that echoes the structural shapes of windows, doors, and stairways. Maintain a consistent color scheme through the entire home. Suggest harmony by arranging objects in paired groupings. Seemingly small details can go a long way in easing family conflicts. Simply placing matching chairs side by side may help soothe a troubled marriage.

■ Where to Begin

Encourage Harmony

When conflict and discord upset family life:

- Arrange rooms and furnishings to avoid conflicts and collisions; keep central spaces and passageways open.
- Select a family color and incorporate it into the scheme for each room.
- Use area rugs and soft, flowing drapery.
- Set furniture and appliances slightly away from the walls.
- Emphasize circular, oval, and spiral forms.
- Place a symbol of welcome in the front entryway.
- Incorporate details drawn from several cultures.
- Display objects in paired groupings.
- Provide subdued lighting; avoid harsh, bright lights.
- Create inviting communal spaces to invite dialog.

"Nothing can bring you peace but yourself."

Ralph Waldo Emerson (1803–1882), U.S. poet and essayist

opposite *Suggesting the archetypal symbol for life's eternal cycle, twisting spiral forms are expressed in this staircase and echoed in the framed artwork. In many traditions, a set of two matching chairs represents marital harmony.*

In Times of Loss . . .

Surely there is no stress so devastating as loss. The end of a relationship, divorce, unemployment, failing health, sudden disability—many events can shake us from the lives we used to call "normal." Perhaps the greatest loss that one can bear is the death of a beloved partner, a child, or a friend. Even the loss of a pet can turn our world upside down.

When you are grieving, it is especially important to make sure that your home feels nurturing and life affirming. Find comfort in solid, earthen things; surround yourself with unpainted wood, rough-hewn stone, and deep red brick. Decorate abundantly with living plants in handcrafted pottery. A ceiling-high ficus tree and hanging pots of Boston fern will bring their own quiet energy into your space. Also, don't forget the healing power of animal companions. While you may not feel ready to take on the responsibility of a dog or cat, now is a good time to start an aquarium or place a bird feeder outside your window.

■ **Where to Begin**

Evoke Nature

During times of loss:

- Surround yourself with wood, stone, clay, and other reminders of nature.
- Use warm, earthy colors—browns, greens, golds, and deep russet.
- Decorate abundantly with living plants.
- Choose fabrics and materials that tantalize the sense of touch; mingle rugged stone with soft velvet, cool marble with shimmering silk.
- Gradually remove items that evoke painful memories; move at your own pace.
- Design with water: Create a tabletop fountain or an indoor pond.
- Start an aquarium or place a bird feeder outside your window.
- Install full-spectrum light fixtures in darker rooms.
- Seek eco-friendly materials that are biodegradable and recyclable.
- Create a home sanctuary for meditation and reflection.

opposite Brick, wood, and rich, earthy colors combine in this comforting seating area. On the sofa, velvet pillows and an embroidered throw add an enticing touch of luxury and warmth.

"The soul would have no rainbow had the eyes no tears."

John Vance Cheney (1895–1919), U.S. poet

"Preserve the old, but know the new."

Chinese proverb

above Meaningful objects are more than merely decorative. In this sunny bedroom, animal sculptures are
carefully placed to inspire dreams and to symbolically
evoke their own special energies. The bed with its
vivid fuchsia covers radiates an aura of tropical adventure and celebrates the possibility for new beginnings.

In Times of New Beginnings . . .

As predictable as the ebb and flow of the tides, cycles of change are part of our everyday lives. Growth from childhood to adolescence to middle age seems to happen all too quickly. Whether changes are anticipated or come to us by surprise, life's transitions can leave us feeling unsettled and disoriented. New marriages, new homes, new neighborhoods, new jobs, new babies, new relationships may be cause for celebration, yet they will also arouse fear and anxiety.

Decorative details that symbolize strength will help you feel more secure during times of transition. Take this opportunity to experiment with exciting new colors, patterns, and details. Choose furnishings and arrangements that can be quickly adapted. Discard nonessentials, but display artifacts passed down from your grandparents or artwork that reflects your cultural heritage. These will help ground you in time and space as you move forward. Appreciate transition as a part of life's adventure. Consider holding a family ceremony to commemorate life's passages: light candles, burn incense, and sing, chant, or play musical instruments.

■ **Where to Begin**

Embrace Change

During times of transition:

- Remove bulky carpeting and draperies.
- Choose lightweight tropical woods.
- Arrange furnishings for easy accessibility.
- Suggest a spirit of adventure with bright, daring colors.
- Bring in exotic orchids or tropical bird-of-paradise flowers.
- Include artwork that will remind you of your heritage or family history.
- Add wicker, cane, and straw accents.
- Hang wind chimes in the windows.
- Burn incense and naturally scented candles.
- Keep in mind the power of numbers: Cluster decorative items in groups of three, six, or nine.

🌳 | **serenity secret #49**

Make lists. Write down the things you must do today and put the most urgent tasks at the top. Also record long-range goals: where you hope to be next month, next year, and five years from today. Even if you don't achieve everything you'd like, you'll feel more in control. Plus, you'll feel a satisfying sense of accomplishment each time you cross an item off your list.

Create a Serenity Zone

A home that soothes and heals is not created overnight. You may find yourself making many changes before one small shift—a bright pillow tossed onto the sofa, a vase of branches beside a window, a brighter bulb in the hallway lamp—creates an entirely new atmosphere. Perhaps you will sense a wave of serenity the moment you step across your threshold. Or, awareness may dawn gradually as you awaken to soul-warming sunlight, feeling unusually calm and deeply rested.

In mystical and spiritual thought, the ideal is to move beyond worldly worries to a transcendent state, a sense of oneness with the universe. Zen Buddhists know it as *satori,* spiritual leaders from India describe *advaita,* while Quakers speak of sensing the *inner light*. On a more pragmatic level, creative artists often refer to a magical state of mind when ideas and inspiration seem to flow from pen or brush. Musicians sometimes speak of being in another dimension when they are truly in tune with the music, playing notes that are not merely correct but in synch with something otherworldly. Athletes use the phrase "in the zone" to describe the magical place where the golfer has a perfect swing, the basketball player scores on every shot, and the baseball player knows instinctively what pitch is coming and wills the bat to strike dead center.

Designing spaces in our homes is a way of reaching for a type of zone where we can feel safe and protected, loved and loving, creative and productive, and completely at peace. *Feng shui, vástu shástra,* prehistoric rituals, color therapy, aromatherapy, and various other design techniques are all tools to help move us toward that ideal. They become most effective when we use them with an understanding of what our homes mean to us and what changes we need to invite into our lives.

Some psychologists believe that we all have the power to tap into the spiritual realm known as the superconscious. It is quite possible that redesigning our interiors can help us attain a new vision of the ordinary, where simple joys lead to deeper insights, the familiar becomes the inspired, and windows open onto a more peaceful way of life.

Serene Spaces Provide . . .

- *Physical safety*
- *Emotional security*
- *Privacy*
- *Comfort*
- *Flexibility and adaptability*
- *Sensual pleasures*
- *Connection with nature*
- *Creativity and self-expression*
- *A sense of heritage*
- *Hope for the future*
- *Spiritual renewal*

---

serenity secret #50

Open a window. Move a table. Add a beautiful detail that speaks to your soul. Creating a joyful and serene life begins with simple actions. Make just one small change, starting today.

"May the warm winds of Heaven
blow softly on your home,
And the Great Spirit bless all
who enter there.
May your moccasins make happy tracks
in many snows,
And may the rainbow always touch
your shoulder."

Cherokee blessing

above *A vase of branches echoes the trees outside and helps direct the flow of energies through this serene, open space. Abundant sunlight and natural views assure a restful atmosphere.*

BUYER'S GUIDE:
Resources for Creating a Stress~Free Home

Many elements go into creating a serene, stress-free home. The suppliers listed here offer a wide range of products, from decorative accents to fragrances and relaxation tools. Most have worldwide distribution centers or international mail order via the Internet.

ancient wisdoms

Ananda Assisi Coop. a r.l.
Casella Postale 48
06088 Santa Maria degli Angeli (PG)
Italy
075-9148505
(fax) 075-9148506
www.innerlife.it
Products, including Sri Yantras, that enhance the inner spiritual life

Ayurveda Holistic Center
www.ayurvedahc.com
Ayurvedic books, dosha kits, and copper Vedic yantras

FastFengShui
415 Dairy Road #E-144
Kahului, HI 96732 USA
808-891-8488
(fax) 808-891-0065
www.fastfengshui.com
Feng shui–inspired products, aromatherapy to water fountains, including Clutter Clearers

So Inspired
20 St. Christophers Court
102 Junction Road
London N19 5QT
UK
(tel./fax) 020-7263-2727
www.soinspired.com
Gifts of the spirit—aromatherapy, feng shui, chakra balancing, and crystals

Vedic Resource
P.O. Box 926337
Houston, TX 77292 USA
713-290-8715; 1-800-829-2579
(fax) 713-290-8720
www.vedicresource.com
Beads, music, yantras, Vastu workbooks, and Vedic charts

decorative accents

Bhargava and Co.
435/A-1, Shak & Nahar Industrial Estate
Lower Parel, Bombay
400 013, Maharashtra
India
91-22-493-0950
(fax) 91-22-493-0949
www.indianmusicals.com
Musical instruments from India

KISEIDO
2255 29th Street, Suite 4
Santa Monica, CA 90405 USA
800-988-6463
(fax) 310-578-7381
www.kiseido.com
Offers elegant, decorative gameboards for Go, the ancient Yin and Yang game.

The Longaberger Company
One Market Square
1500 East Main Street
Newark, OH 43055 USA
740-322-5900
www.longaberger.com
Handcrafted basketry

Marimekko Oyi
Puusepänkatu 4
00880 Helsinki, Finland
358-9-75871
www.marimekko.fi
To the trade only; clothing, interior decoration, and accessories

Mid-East Mfg.
P.O. Box 1523
Emanabad Road
Sialkot
Pakistan
92 (432) 542029
(fax) 92 (432) 551679
www.mid-east.com.pk
Manufacturers of ancient drums and other instruments

Mejiro Co., Ltd.
3-17-30 Shimo Ochiai, Shinjuku-ku
Tokyo 161 0033
Japan
81-(0)3-3950-0051
(fax) 81-(0)3-3950-5492
www.mejiro-jp.com
www.mejiro-jp.com/eng/e_home.html (English)
Crafters of traditional Shinobue and Shakuhachi, Japanese bamboo flutes

Mauviel
B.P. 28
Route de Caen
50800 Villedieu-les-Poêles
France
33 (0) 2 33 61 00 31
(fax) 33 (0) 2 33 50 74 55
www.mauviel.com
Beautiful and functional cooking products

Raja Inc.
3167 San Mateo NE #210
Albuquerque, NM 87110 USA
505-880-0257
(fax) 505-880-0258
www.rajainc2.com
Handmade rugs, baskets, and decor from southwestern USA

Red Eagle Gallery
1034 SW Taylor Street
Portland, OR 97205 USA
503-827-8551
(fax) 503-827-8597
www.redeaglegallery.com
Sculpture, batiks, and baskets from Zimbabwe

Ruffoni
Via Magenta, 5
P.O. Box 11
28887 Omegna VB
Italy
39-0323-61990
(fax) 39-0323-866109
www.ruffonionline.com
Classic Italian copper products for the kitchen and home

Salamó
Padró, 54
17100 La Bisbal d Empord
(GIRONA)
Spain
(tel./fax) 972640255
www.salamoceramica.com
Manufacturer of traditional pottery for
domestic use since the eighteenth century

Sambuco Mario & C. snc
Via della Tecnica
06053 Deruta (PG) I
Italy
39 075 9711625
(fax) 39 075 9711750
www.sambuco.it
Artistic ceramics, majolica, and
terra-cotta pottery

Serenity Health
PMB 49
P.O. Box 7530
Yelm, WA 98597 USA
888-890-5764
(fax) 360-894-0785
www.serenityhealth.com
Handcrafted indoor water fountains, tabletop
fountains, and waterfalls

Spiegel
800-527-1577
www.spiegel.com
Accent tables and chairs, storage, and
decorative items

WANDOO Didgeridoo
38 Curedale Street
Beaconsfield WA 6162
Australia
(08) 9336 2128
www.wadidge.com.au
Authentic Australian didgeridoos, ancient
Aboriginal instruments

Zimmer + Rohde
Zimmersmühlenweg 14-16
61440 Oberursel/Frankfurt
Germany
49 6171 632 02
www.zimmer-rohde.com
To the trade only; silks, transparent fabrics,
and pile weaves

bath and spa

Belhydro
Zwaaikomstraat 72
8800 Roeselare, Belgium
32 (0)51 24 05 08
(fax) 32 (0)51 24 62 80
www.belhydro.be
Whirlpools, bathtubs, steam enclosures, saunas

Kohler
444 Highland Drive
Kohler, WI 53044 USA
800-456-4537
www.kohler.com
Deep soaking tubs and other luxury fixtures

Sanijet
1461 S. Beltline Road, Suite 100
Coppell, TX 75019 USA
972-745-2283
(fax) 972-745-2285
www.sanijet.com
Manufactures pipeless whirlpool tubs

Showerlux U.K. Limited
Sibree Road
Coventry, West Midlands CV3 4FD
UK
(44) (024) 76-639400
(fax) (44) (024) 76-305457
www.duscholux.com
Product line includes combined steam and
shower room

floor coverings

Advance Flooring Company
131 Captain Springs Road Onehunga
P.O. Box 13184
Auckland
New Zealand
09-634-4455 or 0508-238-262
www.ralenti.co.nz/advance
Natural flooring products, including sisal, coir,
seagrass, and leather

The Alternative Flooring Company, Ltd.
Unit 3b Stephenson Close
East Portway Industrial Estate
Andover, Hampshire, SP10 3RU
UK
01264 335111
(fax) 01264 336445
www.alternative-flooring.co.uk
Natural fiber flooring products, including jute,
sisal, wool, seagrass, and coir

Eco-Friendly Flooring
100 S. Baldwin Street, Suite 110
Madison, WI 53703 USA
608-698-0571; 866-250-3273
(fax) 608-834-9000
www.ecofriendlyflooring.com
Wholesale supplier of cork, bamboo, sisal,
and hemp flooring, recycled glass tile, nontoxic
decking, and granite countertops

Sisal Rugs Direct
888-613-1335
www.sisalrugs.com
Custom maker of natural fiber area rugs
in the USA

furnishings and storage

California Closets
www.calclosets.com
Customized storage solutions; worldwide
distribution

Carolina Morning Designs
5790 Highway 80 South
Burnsville, NC 28714 USA
888-267-5366
www.zafu.net
Designs and manufactures traditional
meditation furniture

Harmony In Design
2050 S. Dayton Street
Denver, CO 80231 USA
303-337-7728
(fax) 303-337-8247
www.harmonyindesign.com
Yoga, meditation, and ergonomic furniture

IKEA
www.ikea.com
Simple ergonomic furniture designs; worldwide
distribution

Laura Ashley Ltd
27 Bagleys Lane
Fulham, SW6 2QA
UK
0870 562 2116
www.lauraashley.com
Occasional furniture, wardrobes, bedding,
and curtains

Maine Cottage Furniture
207-846-1430
(fax) 207-846-0602
www.mainecottage.com
Flexible painted wood furnishings

Roche-Bobois
www.roche-bobois.com
Practical furnishings that reflect a blend of
periods and styles

R.O.O.M.
Alstromergaten 20, Box 49024
SE-100 28 Stockholm
Sweden
(46) 8-692-5000
(fax) (46) 8-692-5060
www.room.se
Flexible, functional furnishings, storage,
and decorative accents

Sentient
244 Fifth Avenue, Suite 2117
New York, NY 10010 USA
(tel./fax) 212-772-0112
www.meditationchair.com
Meditation chairs and other ergonomic
furnishings

fragrance, incense, and essential oils

Audrey Leigh Essential Oils
The Old Creamery, Gelli Lane,
Nannerch CH7 5QR
UK
(44) 01352-741-511
(fax) (44) 01352-741-838
www.audreyleigh.com
Therapeutic-quality essential oils

Baieido Co., Ltd.
1-1-4 Kurumano-cho Higashi, Sakai City,
Osaka 590-0943,
Japan
072-229-4545
(fax) 072-227-1672
www.baieido.co.jp/english
Baieido Japanese incense

BIOSUN GmbH
35641 Schwalbach
P.O. Box 100
Germany
49 64 45 / 60 07-0
(fax) 49 64 45 / 60 07-600
www.biosun.de
*Hopi and essential-oil ear candles, relaxation
CDs, and lotions*

The Essential Oil Company
1719 SE Umatilla Street
Portland, OR 97202 USA
800-729-5912
In Oregon: 503-872-8772
(fax) 503-872-8767
www.essentialoil.com
*Unscented lotions that may be combined with
various essential oils*

The Essential Oil Company Ltd
Worting House
Church Lane, Basingstoke
Hampshire RG23 8PX
UK
01256 332 737
(fax) 01256 332 119
www.eoco.org.uk/
*Essential oils, burners, books, magnotherapy
products, and aromatherapy accessories*

New Directions Aromatics
21-B Regan Road
Brampton, Ontario L7A 1C5
Canada
905-840-5459; 877-255-7692
(fax) 905-846-1784
www.poyanaturals.com/
Wildcrafted essential oils

Nutraceutic, Inc.
P.O. Box 358331
Gainesville, FL 32635-8331 USA
888-543-9294; 352-371-3735
(fax) 815-301-8667
www.thenagchampacompany.com
*Online broker of Satya Sai Baba Nag
Champa Indian soaps, incense, and
aromatherapy products*

lighting

Duro-Test Lighting
12401 McNulty Road, Suite 101
Philadelphia, PA 19154 USA
800-289-3876
(fax) 888-959-7250
www.durotest.com
*Designer of Vita-Lite, a fluorescent lamp that
simulates natural daylight*

Environmental Lighting Concepts
P.O. Box 172425
Tampa, FL 33672-0425 USA
813-621-0058; 800-842-8848
(fax) 813-626-8790
www.ott-lite.com
*Developers of OTT-LITE products, made from a
blend of earth phosphors*

Full Spectrum Solutions
4880 Brooklyn Road
Jackson, MI 49201 USA
888-574-7014
(fax) 517-764-4029
www.fullspectrumsolutions.com
www.paralite.com
*Makers of ParaLite and UltraLux brand full-
spectrum lamps with low mercury*

OneTech, L.L.C.
23 Acorn Street
Providence, RI 02903 USA
401-273-5316; 877-663-8324; 514-984-6340
(fax) 401-273-0630
www.onetech.net
*Developer of the Eclipse Computer light, which
helps reduce eyestrain and computer vision
syndrome (CVS)*

Verilux
9 Viaduct Road
Stamford, CT 06907 USA
203-921-2430; 800-786-6850
(fax) 203-921-2427
www.verilux.net
*Lighting products that simulate the full
spectrum of natural light*

relaxation tools

Amida
P.O. Box 1058
Nevada City, CA 95959 USA
800-292-4057
(fax) 530-265-4704
www.ami-da.com
*Online store for meditation supplies, yoga
products, and ceremonial teas*

Arcturus Star Products
25401 County Road F
Cortez, CO 81321 USA
970-564-5811; 888-730-1053
(fax) 970-564-5812
www.arcturusstar.com
*Products that balance the human bioenergy
system by harmonious vibrations*

Askland Technologies, Inc
P.O. Box 2620
Victorville, CA 92393 USA
800-542-7782; 760-949-7678
(fax) 760-949-7868
www.zen-clocks.com
*Zen clocks with a gentle, progressive
alarm function*

BioWaves, LLC.
14150 NE 20th Street, Suite 121
Bellevue, WA 98007 USA
425-895-0050; 800-734-3588
www.biowaves.com
*Designer of tools for vocal analysis and
low-frequency sound therapy*

Brighten Color Flame Candles, Inc.
5125 Convoy Street, Suite 201
San Diego, CA 92111 USA
858-277-2263
www.brightencolorflame.com
*Designer, manufacturer, and retailer of
colored-flame lamp oils and candles*

The Center for Neuroacoustic Research
701 Garden View Court
Encinitas, CA 92024 USA
760-942-6749
(fax) 760-942-6768
www.neuroacoustic.com
*Scientific sound-therapy products, including the
Ergonomic Zero-Gravity Acoustic Vibration
Recliner, sound-therapy tables, goggles, and CDs*

Gaiam Relaxation Company
360 Interlocken Boulevard, Suite 300
Broomfield, CO 80021 USA
303-222-3600
(fax) 303-222-3700
www.therelaxationcompany.com
*Musical and spoken-word relaxation and
meditation programs*

HoMedics, Inc.
3000 Pontiac Trail, Department 168
Commerce Township, MI 48390 USA
800-HOMEDICS (800-466-3342)
www.homedics.com/
*Massagers, aromatherapy, sound therapy, and
other personal-wellness products*

Pacific Light
2212 Queen Anne Avenue N #322
Seattle, WA 98109 USA
877-835-0838
www.healing-peace.com
*Audio and videotapes for relaxation,
meditation, and healing*

Sound Therapy International
P.O. Box A2237
Sydney South NSW 1235
Australia
61-2-9665-1777
(fax) 61-2-9664-9777
www.soundtherapyinternational.com
Self-help sound-therapy program

TenRen
380 Swift Avenue, Suite 5
South San Francisco, CA 94080 USA
650-583-1044
www.tenren.com
Chinese tea products

Theta Technologies
877-4FASHION
www.hypnopage.com
*Light and sound machines for adjusting
mental focus*

Photographers

Courtesy of Laura Ashley
Ltd./www.laurashley.com, 39; 68; 78; 117;
118; 151

Todd Caverly, Brian Vanden Brink Photos/Luigi
Bartolomeo, Architect, 51

Guillaume DeLaubier, 7; 8; 47; 55; 147

Carlos Domenech/Michael Wolk, Design, 43;
155

Tria Giovan, 25; 29; 30; 84; 88; 99; 112; 121;
122

Reto Guntli, 35; 45; 49; 56; 125; 127; 141

John Edward Linden/Fernau & Hartman
Architects, 37

Courtesy of Maine Cottage
Furniture/www.mainecottage.com, 11; 20; 24;
58; 65; 95

Courtesy of Roche-Bobois/www.roche-
bobois.com, 26; 40; 60; 91; 101; 102; 133; 152

Courtesy of R.O.O.M./www.room.se, 62; 74; 85;
98; 113; 130; 131; 138

Eric Roth, 4; 14; 17; 19; 34; 36; 66; 72;
75 (bottom); 76; 77; 79; 83; 93; 96; 100;
139

Tim Street-Porter/www.beateworks.com,
81; 87; 114; 124

Brian Vanden Brink, 22; 23; 129; 135; 136; 137;
142; 145; 149

Brian Vanden Brink/Stephen Blatt, Architect, 71

Brian Vanden Brink/Axel Berg, Builder &
Morningstar Marble & Granite, 146

Brian Vanden Brink/Design Group Three,
Architect & Christina Oliver Interior Design, 107

Brian Vanden Brink/Dominic Merca Dante,
Architect, 104

Brian Vanden Brink/Elliott & Elliott Architects,
41

Brian Vanden Brink/Christina Oliver Interior
Design, 153

Brian Vanden Brink/Quinn Evans, Architect, 111

Brian Vanden Brink Photos/Winton Scott
Architect, 61

Courtesy of Zimmer + Rohde,
Textile manufacturers of three different lines:
Ardecora, Etamine and Zimmer + Rohde, 3; 12;
52; 53; 70; 75 (top)

About the Author

Jackie Craven is a widely published writer who specializes in architecture and interior design. She is the author of *The Healthy Home,* from Rockport Publishers, a columnist for *House & Garden* magazine, and a correspondent for the architecture pages at About.com. Passionate about historic buildings, Jackie finds peace and joy in restoring Victorian houses on her street in upstate New York. Visit her online at www.jackiecraven.com.